LEVERAGING ADVANCES IN SOCIAL NETWORK THINKING FOR NATIONAL SECURITY

PROCEEDINGS OF A WORKSHOP

Julie Anne Schuck, *Rapporteur*

Board on Behavioral, Cognitive, and Sensory Sciences

Division of Behavioral and Social Sciences and Education

The National Academies of
SCIENCES · ENGINEERING · MEDICINE

THE NATIONAL ACADEMIES PRESS
Washington, DC
www.nap.edu

THE NATIONAL ACADEMIES PRESS 500 Fifth Street, NW Washington, DC 20001

This activity was supported by Contract No. 10003166 between the National Academy of Sciences and The Office of the Director of National Intelligence. Any opinions, findings, conclusions, or recommendations expressed in this publication do not necessarily reflect the views of any organization or agency that provided support for the project.

International Standard Book Number-13:   978-0-309-47382-8
International Standard Book Number-10:   0-309-47382-9
Digital Object Identifier: https://doi.org/10.17226/25057

Additional copies of this publication are available for sale from the National Academies Press, 500 Fifth Street, NW, Keck 360, Washington, DC 20001; (800) 624-6242 or (202) 334-3313; http://www.nap.edu.

Copyright 2018 by the National Academy of Sciences. All rights reserved.

Printed in the United States of America

Suggested citation: National Academies of Sciences, Engineering, and Medicine. (2018). *Leveraging Advances in Social Network Thinking for National Security: Proceedings of a Workshop*. Washington, DC: The National Academies Press. doi: https://doi.org/10.17226/25057.

The National Academies of
SCIENCES • ENGINEERING • MEDICINE

The **National Academy of Sciences** was established in 1863 by an Act of Congress, signed by President Lincoln, as a private, nongovernmental institution to advise the nation on issues related to science and technology. Members are elected by their peers for outstanding contributions to research. Dr. Marcia McNutt is president.

The **National Academy of Engineering** was established in 1964 under the charter of the National Academy of Sciences to bring the practices of engineering to advising the nation. Members are elected by their peers for extraordinary contributions to engineering. Dr. C. D. Mote, Jr., is president.

The **National Academy of Medicine** (formerly the Institute of Medicine) was established in 1970 under the charter of the National Academy of Sciences to advise the nation on medical and health issues. Members are elected by their peers for distinguished contributions to medicine and health. Dr. Victor J. Dzau is president.

The three Academies work together as the **National Academies of Sciences, Engineering, and Medicine** to provide independent, objective analysis and advice to the nation and conduct other activities to solve complex problems and inform public policy decisions. The National Academies also encourage education and research, recognize outstanding contributions to knowledge, and increase public understanding in matters of science, engineering, and medicine.

Learn more about the National Academies of Sciences, Engineering, and Medicine at **www.national-academies.org**.

The National Academies of
SCIENCES · ENGINEERING · MEDICINE

Consensus Study Reports published by the National Academies of Sciences, Engineering, and Medicine document the evidence-based consensus on the study's statement of task by an authoring committee of experts. Reports typically include findings, conclusions, and recommendations based on information gathered by the committee and the committee's deliberations. Each report has been subjected to a rigorous and independent peer-review process and it represents the position of the National Academies on the statement of task.

Proceedings published by the National Academies of Sciences, Engineering, and Medicine chronicle the presentations and discussions at a workshop, symposium, or other event convened by the National Academies. The statements and opinions contained in proceedings are those of the participants and are not endorsed by other participants, the planning committee, or the National Academies.

For information about other products and activities of the National Academies, please visit www.nationalacademies.org/about/whatwedo.

STEERING COMMITTEE ON UNDERSTANDING NETWORKS
FOR NATIONAL SECURITY PURPOSES: A WORKSHOP

KATHLEEN M. CARLEY (*Chair*), School of Computer Science, Institute for Software Research International, Carnegie Mellon University
MATTHEW W. BRASHEARS, Department of Sociology, University of South Carolina
NOSHIR CONTRACTOR, McCormick School of Engineering and Applied Science, School of Communications and the Kellogg School of Management, Northwestern University
EMILY FALK, Annenberg School of Communication, University of Pennsylvania
MARKUS MOBIUS, Microsoft Research
JAMES MOODY, Department of Sociology, Duke University

SUJEETA BHATT, *Study Director*
JULIE ANNE SCHUCK, *Program Officer*
RENÉE L. WILSON GAINES, *Senior Program Assistant*

COMMITTEE ON A DECADAL SURVEY OF SOCIAL AND BEHAVIORAL SCIENCES FOR APPLICATIONS TO NATIONAL SECURITY

PAUL R. SACKETT (*Chair*), Department of Psychology, University of Minnesota
GARY G. BERNTSON, Department of Psychology, The Ohio State University
KATHLEEN M. CARLEY, School of Computer Science, Institute for Software Research International, Carnegie Mellon University
NOSHIR S. CONTRACTOR, McCormick School of Engineering and Applied Science, School of Communications, and the Kellogg School of Management, Northwestern University
NANCY J. COOKE, The Polytechnic School, Fulton Schools of Engineering, Arizona State University
BARBARA ANNE DOSHER, Department of Cognitive Science, University of California, Irvine
JEFFREY C. JOHNSON, Department of Anthropology, University of Florida
SALLIE KELLER, Biocomplexity Institute, Virginia Polytechnic Institute and State University, National Capital Region
DAVID MATSUMOTO, Department of Psychology, College of Science and Engineering, San Francisco State University
CARMEN MEDINA, MedinAnalytics, LLC
FRAN P. MOORE, CENTRA Technology, Inc.
JONATHAN D. MORENO, Perelman School of Medicine, Department of Medical Ethics and Health Policy, University of Pennsylvania
JOY ROHDE, Gerald R. Ford School of Public Policy, University of Michigan
JEFFREY W. TALIAFERRO, Department of Political Science, Tufts University
GREGORY F. TREVERTON, Dornsife College of Letters, Arts, and Sciences, School of International Relations, University of Southern California
JEREMY M. WOLFE, Brigham and Women's Hospital, Departments of Ophthalmology and Radiology, Harvard Medical School

SUJEETA BHATT, *Study Director*
ALEXANDRA BEATTY, *Senior Program Officer*
JULIE ANNE SCHUCK, *Program Officer*
ELIZABETH TOWNSEND, *Research Associate*
RENÉE L. WILSON GAINES, *Senior Program Assistant*

BOARD ON BEHAVIORAL, COGNITIVE, AND SENSORY SCIENCES

SUSAN T. FISKE (*Chair*), Department of Psychology and Woodrow Wilson School of Public and International Affairs, Princeton University
JOHN BAUGH, Department of Arts & Sciences, Washington University in St. Louis
LAURA L. CARSTENSEN, Department of Psychology, Stanford University
JUDY DUBNO, Department of Otolaryngology-Head and Neck Surgery, Medical University of South Carolina
JENNIFER EBERHARDT, Department of Psychology, Stanford University
ROBERT L. GOLDSTONE, Department of Psychological and Brain Sciences, Indiana University
DANIEL R. ILGEN, Department of Psychology, Michigan State University
JAMES S. JACKSON, Institute for Social Research, University of Michigan
NANCY G. KANWISHER, Department of Brain and Cognitive Sciences, Massachusetts Institute of Technology
JANICE KIECOLT-GLASER, Department of Psychology, The Ohio State University College of Medicine
BILL C. MAURER, School of Social Sciences, University of California, Irvine
JOHN MONAHAN, School of Law, University of Virginia
STEVEN E. PETERSEN, Department of Neurology and Neurological Surgery, Washington University School of Medicine
DANA M. SMALL, Department of Psychiatry, Yale Medical School
TIMOTHY J. STRAUMAN, Department of Psychology and Neuroscience, Duke University
JEREMY M. WOLFE, Brigham and Women's Hospital, Departments of Ophthalmology and Radiology, Harvard Medical School

BARBARA A. WANCHISEN, *Director*
THELMA COX, *Program Coordinator*

Acknowledgments

This Proceedings of a Workshop was reviewed in draft form by individuals chosen for their diverse perspectives and technical expertise. The purpose of this independent review is to provide candid and critical comments that will assist the National Academies of Sciences, Engineering, and Medicine in making each published proceedings as sound as possible and to ensure that it meets the institutional standards for quality, objectivity, evidence, and responsiveness to the charge. The review comments and draft manuscript remain confidential to protect the integrity of the process.

We thank the following individuals for their review of this proceedings: Bradley M. Cooke, Directorate for Social, Behavioral, and Economic Sciences, National Science Foundation; Christa Brelsford, Geographic Information Science and Technology Group, Oak Ridge National Laboratory; and James Moody, Department of Sociology, Duke University.

Although the reviewers listed above provided many constructive comments and suggestions, they were not asked to endorse the content of the proceedings, nor did they see the final draft before its release. The review of this proceedings was overseen by Gary LaFree, National Consortium for the Study of Terrorism and Responses to Terrorism, University of Maryland. He was responsible for making certain that an independent examination of this proceedings was carried out in accordance with standards of the National Academies and that all review comments were carefully considered. Responsibility for the final content rests entirely with the rapporteur and the National Academies.

Kathleen M. Carley, *Chair*
Steering Committee on Understanding Networks for
National Security Purposes

Contents

1 **INTRODUCTION**   1
The Decadal Survey of Social and Behavioral Sciences for Applications to National Security, 1
Objectives for the Six Workshops, 3
Introduction to the Workshop on Social Network Thinking, 4
Structure of This Proceedings, 6

2 **NETWORKS-PLUS: BEYOND THE INDIVIDUAL (TEAMS AND CONTEXTS)**   9
Supersynthesizers in an Age of Influence, 10
Organizing in Teams, 12
The Future of Urban Network Research, 14
Use of Crowdsourced Data During Emergencies, 16

3 **NETWORKS-PLUS: WITHIN THE INDIVIDUAL**   19
The Brain in the Social World, 19
The Brain and Social Networks, 21
Emotional Artificial Intelligence, 24
The Study of Identities and Their Impact on Networks, 26

4 **MULTILEVEL, HIGH-DIMENSIONAL, EVOLVING, AND EMERGING NETWORKS**   29
Exploring Dark Networks, 29
Robust Summary Statistics for Networks, 31
The Future of Complex Networks, 33

5 DISCUSSION   37
   Collaboration Networks in the IC, 37
   Areas for Further Research on Networks and Network Thinking, 38
   Data Needs, 41
   Ethical Considerations in Conducting Research on Social
      Networks, 42
   Closing, 43

APPENDIXES

A Statement of Task for the Decadal Survey of Social and Behavioral
   Sciences for Applications to National Security   45
B Workshop Agenda   47
C Participants List   51
D Biographical Sketches of Steering Committee Members and
   Presenters   57

1

Introduction

The Office of the Director of National Intelligence (ODNI), which oversees and directs the work of the 17 agencies and organizations responsible for foreign, military, and domestic intelligence for the United States, has an interest in research from the social and behavioral sciences that may be beneficial to the Intelligence Community (IC). To develop a systematic understanding of these potential benefits, ODNI requested that the National Academies of Sciences, Engineering, and Medicine conduct a decadal survey of the social and behavioral sciences to identify research opportunities that show promise for supporting national security efforts in the next 10 years.

THE DECADAL SURVEY OF SOCIAL AND BEHAVIORAL SCIENCES FOR APPLICATIONS TO NATIONAL SECURITY

A decadal survey is a method for engaging members of a research community to identify lines of research with the greatest potential utility in the pursuit of a particular goal. The National Academies pioneered this type of survey with a study of ground-based astronomy in 1964.[1] Since then, committees appointed by the National Academies have conducted more than 15 decadal surveys. The Decadal Survey of Social and Behavioral Sciences for Applications to National Security represents the first opportunity to apply this approach to the social and behavioral sciences. Its purpose is to develop an understanding of the lines of research in these

---

[1] National Academy of Sciences. (1964). *Ground-Based Astronomy: A Ten-Year Program.* Washington, DC: National Academy Press. doi: https://doi.org/10.17226/13212.[April 2018].

fields that offer the greatest potential to enhance the capabilities of the IC. To carry out this work, the National Academies appointed the Committee on the Decadal Survey of Social and Behavioral Sciences for Applications to National Security (Decadal Survey Committee); the committee's charge appears in Appendix A.

The Decadal Survey Committee has pursued many avenues in collecting information about the needs of the IC and relevant cutting-edge research in the social and behavioral sciences. As part of its information-gathering process, the committee held a series of six workshops—the first three on October 11, 2017, and the second three on January 24, 2018.[2] These workshops, for which planning began early in the committee process, were designed to explore areas about which the committee wished to learn more and to allow the committee to engage with a broad range of experts. The topics selected for the workshops do not necessarily indicate the ultimate direction of the committee's deliberations. The six topics addressed by the workshops were

1. changing sociocultural dynamics and implications for national security;
2. emerging trends and methods in international security;
3. leveraging advances in social network thinking for national security;
4. learning from the science of cognition and perception for decision making;
5. workforce development and intelligence analysis; and
6. understanding narratives for national security purposes.

Separate steering committees, whose membership included both members of the Decadal Survey Committee and additional experts in the topics to be addressed, were appointed to plan these workshops. Each of these committees was guided by its own charge. All were asked to bring their expertise to bear in identifying specific areas of promising research and experts with deep knowledge who could offer a range of insights.

This Proceedings of a Workshop, prepared by the workshop rapporteur, summarizes the presentations and discussions at the third workshop, which addressed advances in social network thinking.[3] This workshop was planned by the Steering Committee on Understanding Networks for National Security Purposes, whose charge is presented in Box 1-1. The workshop's purpose was to explore the current state of research on social

---

[2] For more information about the Decadal Survey and all of the workshops, see http://nas.edu/SBSDecadalSurvey [January 2018].

[3] For the archived Webcast of the workshop and available presentations, see http://sites.nationalacademies.org/DBASSE/BBCSS/DBASSE_181267 [November 2017].

> **BOX 1-1**
> **Workshop Steering Committee Charge**
>
> An ad hoc steering committee will plan and conduct a 1-day public workshop. The workshop will feature invited presentations and discussions to understand how network thinking will evolve and transform the Intelligence Community in the next 10 years. The committee will plan and organize the workshop, select speakers and discussants, and moderate the discussions at the workshop. The workshop will be part of a set of workshops designed to gather information for the Decadal Survey of Social and Behavioral Sciences for Applications to National Security. A Proceedings of the Workshop will be prepared by a designated rapporteur in accordance with institutional guidelines.

network thinking that has relevance for national security. It should be noted that the steering committee's role was limited to planning and convening the workshop, and that the views contained in this proceedings are those of individual workshop participants and do not necessarily represent the views of all workshop participants, the steering committee, or the National Academies. The agenda for the workshop appears in Appendix B; a list of individuals who attended the three workshops held on October 11, 2017, is presented in Appendix C; and biographical sketches of the steering committee members and speakers are provided in Appendix D.

OBJECTIVES FOR THE SIX WORKSHOPS

In an opening session for the three October 11, 2017, workshops, the chair of the Decadal Survey Committee, Paul Sackett, University of Minnesota, and sponsor representative David Honey, ODNI, provided background information on the objectives for the six workshops.

Sackett observed that the Decadal Survey Committee will rely heavily on input from experts in the communities of national security and behavioral and social science research. Given the breadth of the committee's charge, he explained, it must cast a wide net, extending well beyond the specific expertise of its members. He described the six workshops as an important part of the effort to gather ideas. The workshops would support the committee by helping to identify promising research areas and allowing the committee members to engage in discussion with experts in a wide range of areas salient to its work.[4]

Honey expressed appreciation to all those contributing to the committee's work through the workshops and other activities, noting that the participation of the full range of experts in the intelligence and behavioral and social science communities would be needed to make the decadal study successful. Making predictions about future directions for research is difficult, he acknowledged, but in his view it is necessary. He noted that the final report of the Decadal Survey Committee will be "a very powerful tool" for government officials who must make decisions regarding funding and other priorities. The decadal model, he explained, "offered the best opportunity" to identify research directions and priorities that reflect a wide range of insights and perspectives. "Decision makers are really asking much deeper and more probing questions today than we've seen before," he said. "They really want to know why surprising movements such as the Arab Spring [uprisings that began in 2010] occur. The national security community is eager for new ways to understand such events and how to respond to them, and also for better ways to assess their interventions after the fact." Honey thanked the participants for contributing, emphasizing that their ideas would be "crucial for getting us where we need to go."

INTRODUCTION TO THE WORKSHOP ON SOCIAL NETWORK THINKING

The workshop steering committee recognized that advancing technology is changing the environment in which humans reside, and that these changes are in turn influencing the way social networks form and evolve, as well as how they might be studied. Scholars in many disciplines have developed theories and research strategies to pursue understanding of these changes, and also to utilize an unprecedented availability of data. Researchers are applying their evolving approaches to address a range of social phenomena and problems. To explore this range of work, the committee invited presenters to describe research that applies social network thinking to several areas of inquiry. Presenters were instructed to consider recent advances in their areas of work and the gains that could be made with future investment.

Committee chair Kathleen Carley, Carnegie Mellon University, explained that a primary goal for the workshop was to explore ways to "reason about and understand relations among things, people, organiza-

---

[4] Other activities associated with the Decadal Survey include calls for white papers, public meetings, and an online discussion forum; see http://nas.edu/SBSDecadalSurvey [December 2017].

tions, and ideas" and how that understanding can support intelligence decisions. She provided an overview of social network thinking and some of the challenges related to methods and data used in studying networks. She noted that the science of social networks has expanded: the tools and data sources available today are quite different from those of the past. The field has relied on surveys of small groups of people that identify the various relationships within an organization or community, and those methods are still used, she acknowledged, but attention has shifted to ever larger datasets and networks.

Carley added that new technologies, such as those developed for automated communications, machine learning, psychological profiling, speech analysis, and video modification, are changing the ways in which social networks are formed and investigated. However, she asserted, these advances are not without challenges. One such challenge is that these technological advances are also increasing opportunities for "enhanced disinformation" about what is really going on within a given network and among whom. For example, Carley noted, advances in voice and image software are opening up the possibility of generating fabricated images and videos of conversations between people that appear to be real, even though they never occurred. She added that machine-driven bots or cyborgs (humans who use bot technology) can create the illusion of human interaction in online networks, as well as introduce propaganda into online discussions.[5] She noted that producing credible analyses of social networks when the underlying interaction data may be suspect is a challenge.

Carley introduced three terms used within the community of researchers on social network thinking: "echo chamber," "superspreader," and "superfriend." An "echo chamber" refers to a network of actors who are densely connected in at least two ways: they are in frequent communication with each other, and they use shared terms or address a shared set of topics. Within echo chambers, information, ideas, and beliefs diffuse rapidly and are amplified and reinforced within the network. A "superspreader" is someone who can send information widely to numerous individuals, directly or indirectly. When an idea is mentioned by a superspreader, it is likely to be "heard" by many others. Finally, a "superfriend" is someone who is involved in numerous reciprocal relationships and is critical in engaging groups through ongoing dialogue. Carley noted that these three

---

[5] Carley gave the example of the FiribiNome bot to illustrate why new network thinking tools are needed and being developed. One of the echo chamber bots associated with ISIS could not be discovered using traditional social network metrics. Within the Twitter platform, sophisticated use of @mentions through the bot made it possible to grow networked communities, promote accounts, and gain influence on these communities. Once the bot had manipulated Twitter recommendations and grown a community of followers, it promoted a site for the collection of money for children of Syria that was actually a money-laundering site for ISIS.

concepts have been in use for some time and that researchers have validated ways of measuring them. She pointed out that these concepts are important to the types of social networks observed today, such as those in social media. However, she observed, the traditional measures may not be suited to analysis of new data on networks given the volume of the data and their time-variant nature, and more complex dynamic metrics are needed.

Accordingly, Carley reported, the science of social networks today is making use of data from remote sensors and such techniques as machine learning, big data analytics, and neural imaging to investigate people's behaviors within social networks. She explained that the social media landscape has created new types of networks to which vast amounts of data are tied, and researchers are eager to use this wealth of data to advance social network thinking. However, the challenges she had alluded to earlier complicate what questions can be investigated with these data and what can be known about these social networks. In addition to the challenges previously cited, she observed that sampling biases may be introduced when companies or data providers limit access to some data and when legal authorities limit the collection and storage of certain data.

Carley explained that the workshop would consider two emerging notions of the science of social networks that have come to be referred to as "networks-plus" and "complexity." The term "networks-plus" refers to research that goes beyond the simplified view of "who-to-whom" connections in a network to consider the contexts associated with or external influences on that network, as well as the contributions of physiological, psychological, and cognitive factors that influence the individual network members. The term "complexity," she said, refers to two additional approaches: (1) the study of new forms of large, global online networks; and (2) the effort to use network thinking for forecasting and predicting future actions, rather than just for purposes of description and comparison.

STRUCTURE OF THIS PROCEEDINGS

This proceedings follows the structure of the workshop. Chapter 2 summarizes four workshop presentations on the external influences on networks (an aspect of networks-plus research). These presentations covered assembling analytic teams of supersynthesizers,[6] team organization, urban network research, and the use of crowdsourced data. Chapter 3 turns to research on the individual and internal factors of networks (another aspect of networks-plus research). It summarizes two presentations on the relation

---

[6] As described in Chapter 2, supersynthesizers are people with cognitive and analytic skills beyond those of "superforecasters," a term that refers to people identified as the most accurate in determining future geopolitical and economic outcomes.

INTRODUCTION

of brain functioning and social networks and two other presentations on emotional artificial intelligence and the study of social identities. The three presentations summarized in Chapter 4 addressed complexity in terms of "multilevel, high-dimensional, evolving, and emerging networks," examining the exploration of dark networks, robust summary statistics for networks, and the future of complex networks. Finally, Chapter 5 summarizes the discussions between presenters and other workshop participants on the topics raised during the workshop, focusing on collaboration networks in the IC, areas for further research on networks and network thinking, data needs, and ethical considerations in conducting research on social networks.

2

Networks-Plus: Beyond the Individual (teams and contexts)

The first workshop panel focused on using networks to understand the functioning of individuals in the context of the social and physical worlds. Matthew Brashears, University of South Carolina, a moderator of this panel, raised several points about networks to start the session. First, he suggested that physical proximity can be an ambiguous signal; that is, physical closeness does not necessarily indicate that individuals have a significant interaction or relationship. Second, he observed that electronic devices designed to serve as sensors, tracking locations and other types of data, can also lead to interactions and modify individuals' behaviors. For example, people may use these technologies for "impression management," using them strategically to achieve particular objectives and even introducing a degree of deception in the information that is captured.

Brashears also referenced the large amount of data collected through physical sensors and online interactions that can be used for network studies. He suggested that researchers think not only about data they can collect but also data they can scrap. The challenge today, he elaborated, is not finding data; rather, the challenge is identifying the theoretical and methodological approaches best suited to sorting through the data to find what is most useful for insights on network thinking.

Brashears emphasized that what is considered to be a network, as well as how that network is measured, depends fundamentally on the context in which research on the network is conducted. He cited three different types of context: geographic, political, and cultural. Relationships, he said, often depend on proximity with respect to these contexts. That is, connections are made when one person comes in contact with another, physically or virtually, and stronger connections result when the two share cultural knowledge or political ideas. One challenge today, according to Brashears, is to understand the echo chambers created by social media algorithms that intentionally connect people with similar interests, and how they are changing the ways in which social networks are formed and used to achieve individual and social goals.

SUPERSYNTHESIZERS IN AN AGE OF INFLUENCE

Regina Joseph, New York University, described her research on supersynthesizers, defined as individuals with cognitive and analytic skills that go beyond those of superforecasters.[1] Superforecasters, she explained, are individuals identified as "most accurate in determining future geopolitical and economic outcomes." She argued that supersynthesizers are needed as members of analytic teams within the Intelligence Community (IC) to tackle national security challenges presented by the changing nature of social networks and the ways in which the public retrieves, consumes, and distributes information. In the past, she suggested, the influence of information could be represented by a "one-to-many broadcast model," with information being distributed through radio, television, and print, whereas today, the addition of social media and global networks has resulted in a "many-to-many broadcast model." This new model presents challenges, she said, because of its speed, ease of access, and vulnerability to entrenching confirmation biases (the echo chamber effect noted by Brashears).

Joseph continued by asserting that society is at a point where technology for documenting truth is about to be superseded by technology for fabricating deception. She elaborated that society and the security community have become accustomed to a level of protection afforded by technologies that record images and sound (e.g., security cameras). Increasingly, however, that protection is being questioned as people develop and use technologies and software programs to create fake images, to mimic sounds of people speaking, and to simulate videos (i.e., generating audio, recording faces, and mapping them together to create the illusion of a captured speech or interaction on video that never actually occurred). Through this growing ability to fabricate digital information, Joseph argued, societies across the globe face greater difficulty in distinguishing between reality and false narratives. They are subject to more intrusions and influences in the public space via social networks, whether it be propaganda, disinformation, or legitimate attempts to sway public opinion.

Joseph considered this new information environment through the lens

---

[1]For more information on superforecasting, see Tetlock, P.E., and Gardner, D. (2016). *Superforecasting: The Art and Science of Prediction.* New York: Broadway Books.

of Aldous Huxley, who wrote of an ultimate revolution whereby "control takes place through willing participation on the part of the individuals." She used the example of Facebook, where vast numbers of individuals have knowingly given up their privacy and some security in exchange for the social and informational transactions enabled by the site. These transactions, she suggested, can have adverse impacts if manipulated for emotional effect. From a Huxley viewpoint, she asserted, the addictive behavior of active social media users constitutes a form of servitude; devotion to such platforms and the enormous amount of personal data now owned by social media companies underscore the potential for effective control of the public.

Joseph expressed concern about the shrinking diversity of information being accessed by members of the public, as well as the increasing risks of disinformation. Such influence, she suggested, may become a threat to national security, warranting consideration of counterinfluences. Identifying appropriate counterinfluences, she continued, requires early detection, which in this new information environment will depend on intelligence analysts' ability to "harness the advantages of open-source information and social networks" and on the development of supports to improve analytic teams' situational awareness and their ability to detect signals in noise.

Joseph suggested that a new type of expertise is needed. She pointed out that the nation's education system privileges vertical specialization and creates a talent pool of specialists with very particular forms of knowledge. Drawing on the McKinsey concept, she identified these specialists as "t-shaped" individuals—those who have in-depth knowledge in one or two areas and skills complementary to other areas.[2] She argued that such individuals are a good start to meeting the needs for expertise, but that the needed expertise would better come from "comb-shaped" individuals—those "who have multiple areas of niched expertise that are connected with long and broad deep generalist knowledge." She explained that this "comb-shaped" concept emerged from the study of superforecasters that identified individuals with superior general knowledge, better resistance to biases, and multiple areas of expertise.

In closing, Joseph identified three areas for future research: (1) research to identify individuals as supersynthesizers, (2) research to develop training that can hone skills for synthesizing information, and (3) research and development to produce hybrid cognitive-assist platforms and technologies to aid humans in their analytic work. She pointed to some avenues of inquiry in her own research that are identifying and targeting these needs: anticipatory intelligence; cognitive prosthetics; and human–machine innovation,

---

[2]For more information, see, for example, https://www.psychologytoday.com/blog/career-transitions/201204/career-success-starts-t [February 2018].

including neurocognitive approaches and analytical quantification using sophisticated crowdsourcing.

ORGANIZING IN TEAMS

Leslie DeChurch, Northwestern University, provided an overview of the research literature on teams and teaming and how teams can be understood from a social network perspective. A primary conclusion from her research, she said, is that "teams assemble from networks to form networks of teams whose success can be predicted by looking at the networks that exist within and between teams." She went on to define several terms salient to her presentation.

First, "teams in organizations" refers to the traditional view of a team as a predefined, relatively small group of people with a clear boundary and shared goal. Second, "organizing in teams" denotes a dynamic group of many more people with a fluid boundary and a shared purpose. Finally, "teaming" is defined as "purposive, collaborative interaction among a set of individuals." In the rest of her presentation, DeChurch identified literature that has examined how to assemble, manage, detect, and/or disrupt teaming.

According to DeChurch, two types of literature in the behavioral sciences—in the areas of team assembly and team composition—address how teams assemble from networks. In the team assembly area, she said, researchers examine what social forces drive people to want to work together. Findings from this research, she continued, indicate that self-forming teams avoid diversity, leading to networks that are often homophilous and face challenges with bringing in newcomers; they avoid becoming too large; and they tend to assemble with previous collaborators. In the team composition area, researchers examine the best team composition for optimal performance. DeChurch observed that findings in this area point to the benefits of diversity—a diverse range of expertise, as well as a balance between newcomers and incumbents. She noted further that what is known about how to design good teams is at odds with what is known about how teams naturally assemble.

DeChurch presented some findings from a recent study of factors affecting the selection of teammates among environmental scientists and social psychologists from two different universities. Participants were given a complex problem to address, along with a recommender system that algorithmically identified potential collaborators. DeChurch reported that these scientists were most likely to team up with prior collaborators. Those not choosing prior collaborators were more likely to team up with a "recommended teammate" (someone in the top 10 from the recommender system) as opposed to a random selection. DeChurch pointed out that the algorithmic teammate recommendations significantly improved the chances of teaming up for those who had not previously collaborated.

DeChurch continued to point to relevant literature, such as that in the area of multiteam systems, team interaction networks, and leadership networks (how teaming is managed). She defined a multiteam system as a network comprising two or more teams that pursue both proximal team subgoals and distal system-level goals. Research in this area, she noted, has shown that leadership that fosters connections within and between teams is an important element of effective multiteam systems. A concept that has emerged in this research, she added, is that of group social capital, defined as the set of informal ties connecting teams to other groups and providing access to people in other agencies or organizations.

DeChurch pointed out that research in the area of team interaction networks has expanded on a long history of literature, largely in psychology, focused on the properties of well-functioning groups and teams. One of the findings from this work, she said, is "that small groups suffer in their ability to share information…so decision biases and heuristics that individuals hold when they process information only get further magnified when people [stay confined to a small group]." She noted that information sharing and decision making improve among teams with decentralized information-sharing networks.

Research in the area of leadership networks, DeChurch observed, has examined both formal and informal leadership. The findings from this work indicate that teams with formal leaders who are more central (i.e., have many connections outside the team) are more effective than teams with less central leaders. DeChurch added that the work on teams with informal leadership (i.e., teams with few if any prescribed leaders) has found that such teams still need individuals to assume the role of providing motivation and direction for the group, and that those informal leaders with "dense influence ties" improve the effectiveness of their teams. She suggested that the reason outside or multiteam connections are important is that they improve information sharing, which in turn can bring more facts and ideas to teams for consideration, as well as increase understanding of and appreciation for a team's progress and goals.

DeChurch drew attention to one study that examined how prompts or interventions affect information sharing among online teams. The study found that several interventions changed how teams interacted by increasing the amount of information sharing beyond that resulting from simply instructing team members to collaborate and share unique information. DeChurch explained that the three interventions were developed from the psychological literature on how groups process information: (1) the task was framed as having a demonstrably correct solution; (2) a cooperative norm among the team was created; and (3) participants were instructed to use a structured discussion process. She believes this study was useful because it illustrated the possibility of intervening with teams to improve (or perhaps disrupt) their collaboration.

DeChurch offered some applications of the literature on organizing in teams to the work of intelligence analysts. She referenced a report that reviewed the prewar intelligence reports on Iraq's weapons programs and intelligence oversight after the terrorist attacks of September 11, 2001,[3] which identified shortcomings in teamwork. She cited from that report issues of "groupthink dynamics" that led to assumptions and failure to use institutional mechanisms designed to challenge those assumptions, as well as issues of bureaucratic structure and complex policies that impeded information sharing. These events, she reported, led to calls for reorganizing analytic teams and gaining new knowledge that would help the IC with teaming, enabling analysts to "adaptively configure and reconfigure themselves" as necessary. She pointed to four themes in the literature that are important to the IC community: How can agile analyst teams be *assembled*? How can these teams be *managed*? How do analyst teams *detect* adversarial teams? Finally, how can adversarial teams be *disrupted*?

In closing, DeChurch presented her thoughts on priorities for future research. First, she suggested the development of "support mechanisms that will enable effective team assembly practices and team self-regulatory processes." Second, she offered several research ideas that could provide the foundation for developing these mechanisms: (1) identify the network structures that optimize the performance of analyst teams; (2) validate network interventions; and (3) develop technologies that aid the work of analyst teams.

THE FUTURE OF URBAN NETWORK RESEARCH

Zachary Neal, Michigan State University, provided an overview of research on urban networks, drawing on events at a recent symposium in Belgium sponsored by the Urban Studies Foundation. He described the symposium as bringing together 40 scholars in both the social and natural sciences from around the world to discuss a future research agenda at the intersection of urban studies and network science. He commented that the field of urban network research has grown in size and scope in the last decade. Participants at the symposium represented several different disciplines and areas of expertise: those in physics and mathematics specialize in big data and methodological sophistication; those in geography specialize in

---

[3] Rosenbach, E., and Peritz, A.J. (2009). *Confrontation or Collaboration? Congress and the Intelligence Community.* Boston, MA: Harvard Kennedy School, Belfer Center for Science and International Affairs.

understanding and modeling spatial data; those in sociology specialize in understanding human behavior and the formation of groups; and those in urban planning specialize in the practical effects of infrastructure and urban policy.

Neal offered a quote from the work of Michael Batty to express the importance of research in urban networks: "To understand place, we must understand flows, and to understand flows, we must understand networks." Neal explained that places are where events happen, and that to forecast events, one must have a better understanding of networks to make sense of the flow of ideas and behaviors that affect events.

Neal helped the audience understand the nature of an urban network by identifying some of its features. The entities or nodes in an urban network can be, for example, people, road intersections, or cities. The connections or ties between the nodes can be financial, human, or commodity flows. The scale of an urban network can be within a city or among multiple cities. Neal pointed out that the research on urban networks has been characterized by an overreliance on node-level analysis as opposed to analysis at other levels (e.g., the dyadic, or pairs of nodes, level and the network level). However, he added, the field has made use of multiple layers in its analyses; given information from geographic information systems, for example, street networks can be overlaid on social networks.

According to Neal, the symposium had made clear that the field of urban networks is conducting research relevant to the IC. This includes (1) economic work to identify global and regional economic patterns and understand how and why those patterns are changing over time; (2) transportation research to ensure accessibility from one place to another, but also to understand the robustness of systems under failure or attack; (3) investigations of online social networks to track (via geotagged posts) the spatial diffusion of illnesses or ideas; and (4) research on communities that examines where people live and travel and how infrastructure affects community cohesion, segregation, and polarization.

Given both the range of questions that arise in urban network research and the number of relevant disciplines, Neal sees a need for researchers to consider more carefully when a network science approach is appropriate for a particular research question to address some of the issues he has noted in the literature. One such issue is that a network is often presented as a naturally occurring thing, when it is in fact a simplification used for conceptual and analytic clarity. Another issue, Neal asserted, is that paths must be meaningful if a matrix of data is to be treated as a network; he argued that correlation matrices and origin–destination matrices are not networks. He suggested the need for minimum reporting standards for publication for those in the field of network science, and urban networks in particular. His ideas included having researchers define both the nodes and edges in their work and demonstrate how they were measured, as well as the validity of those measurements. He also suggested that researchers be required to provide a theoretical justification for why particular nodes and edges together form a network that matters.

Neal called attention to one of the major challenges in the field—whether available network methods work for spatially embedded networks. Many current methods were developed from nonspatial graph theory, he observed, adding that the field has discovered that "conventional community detection algorithms tend to work fairly poorly if the network is spatially embedded." By poorly, he said he meant that the algorithms almost always find the already-obvious proximate clusters of nodes and provide no deeper information. In addition, he said, conventional statistical null models fail to account for the spatial embedding present in most urban network contexts. Furthermore, he said, "Conventional summary statistics . . . used in the network literature like clustering coefficients and path links often don't take into account how those features might be different in spatially embedded networks." He urged researchers to start developing new theoretical and methodological tools.

USE OF CROWDSOURCED DATA DURING EMERGENCIES

Guido Cervone, Pennsylvania State University, provided an overview of what is known as "cyberscience" and then discussed findings from his own research on citizen science[4] efforts following a nuclear emergency in Japan. He pointed out that science has progressed for centuries largely through a combination of observation, theory development, and experimentation. But in the last 30 years, he said, something fundamentally different has been added to the mix—data- or computational-enabled research—to which the label "cyberscience," or in his field "geoinformatics," has recently been given. In Cervone's opinion, this approach "has been transformative" with respect to the way research is undertaken.

Cervone observed that there exist many different types of data and a number of large datasets. He explained that the largest datasets include data from commercial transactions, videos and audio, remote sensing, numerical modeling,[5] and geographic submissions volunteered through social media or online citizen science projects. He then asserted that data are not particularly useful by themselves, and described how data, information, and knowledge differ: data are a collection of symbols and other recorded

---

[4] "Citizen science" refers to science projects that use members of the general public to collect and/or analyze data.

[5] Cervone pointed out, "numerical models generate orders of magnitude of new data from their initial datasets."

material, information is interpreted data, and knowledge is patterns in data used to solve problems. He suggested that the way to get from data to knowledge, particularly with large amounts of data, is by using automated algorithms. These algorithms, he explained, are generally created outside of such fields as geography; they emanate from mathematics, statistics, computer science, and other fields that research databases, machine learning, and artificial intelligence. He expressed his view that in the future, the content and computational fields could work together more closely to develop algorithms needed to solve difficult problems.

Cervone then turned to his research on the reliability of a citizen science contribution to a dataset. He showed satellite images and video of the 2011 nuclear crisis that occurred in Fukushima, Japan, after an earthquake triggered a tsunami that caused a massive failure in the cooling system at a nuclear power plant. He reported that about a month after the event, the U.S. Department of Energy and its Japanese counterpart began collecting remote sensing data to examine the extent of radiation contamination from the accident. These data were collected over a 2-month period and would serve as the official measurements of the radiation. In addition to this government effort, however, there also were unofficial measurements. Cervone explained that in the immediate aftermath of the accident, the University of Tokyo initiated a citizen science project called SAFECAST, which distributed about 8,000 instruments[6] to people living in the Fukushima area so they could collect crowdsourced radiation data. These people became a network of data contributors, and Cervone reported that to date, 70 million of these observations have been uploaded to the SAFECAST server.

Cervone then raised the question of whether data collected by citizens could be useful for national security applications. He reported that by itself, the SAFECAST collection of data tends to overpredict the extent of radiation. However, he explained that the coverage of the citizen data varies widely, with some locations having many observations and others having few (given the mobility of people with instruments). However, his research group has been able to make several interpolations over time to compensate for this variability in the data, and Cervone reported that with this calibration, the distribution in the unofficial data matches well with the official data. He concluded by asserting that citizen collection of data is useful, particularly because it provides continuous measurements beyond what has been collected by official efforts. He warned, however, that spatial and temporal patterns in the collected data may affect what can be known from the data. He also cautioned that this particular dataset is currently publicly accessible but may not be in the future.

---

[6]These instruments were an open-source bGeigie Nano device that uses the LND7317 radiation sensor, which can detect alpha, beta, and gamma radiation.

3

Networks-Plus: Within the Individual

The second workshop panel showcased research focused on understanding how people's cognitive and affective states are influenced by and influence social networks. According to panel moderator Noshir Contractor, Northwestern University, the presentations in this panel represented a new line of research in the area of social network thinking. This research, he said, which combines investigations on cognition, neural influences, and social psychology, presents an opportunity to move beyond identifying the attributes and traits of individuals to examine the physiological underpinnings of individuals' behaviors as a result of social network interactions. He pointed out that research in this area addresses both how social networks influence the mind and how what is occurring inside the mind influences social networks. Emily Falk, University of Pennsylvania, a virtual moderator and presenter in this panel, added that researchers are interested in understanding how people use and perceive their networks, and are looking at individuals' use of social networks from a number of perspectives, such as identity formation and social, cognitive, and affective features.

THE BRAIN IN THE SOCIAL WORLD

Carolyn Parkinson, University of California, Los Angeles, provided examples of studies that integrate approaches from social neuroscience and psychology with those from social network thinking to investigate information processing within individual minds. This integrated work is just beginning, she noted, but shows much promise. She pointed out that previous work in social neuroscience has studied single relationships in isolation, citing the example of studies in which brain responses are compared as individuals view pictures of friends versus strangers. While limited, she said, these studies have provided insight into how individuals process social cues.

Parkinson called attention to the social brain hypothesis in social neuroscience. According to this hypothesis, many distinctive features of the human brain, its size and associated sophisticated cognitive abilities, have evolved specifically to enable humans to track and navigate large complexly bonded social groups. According to Parkinson, it makes sense intuitively that people are embedded in social networks and that the brain must store and retrieve a wide range of social knowledge to manage social interactions effectively on a daily basis. However, she said, little is known from science about the process of inferring and retrieving information about social networks and how such information impacts individuals' thoughts and behaviors. She suggested that integrating approaches from social neuroscience and social network thinking would help elucidate various facets of social networks and their impacts on people's behaviors. She then presented findings from studies that have yielded some preliminary understanding in this area.

One study described by Parkinson examined the social network of a cohort of MBA students. The social network was first characterized by mapping out all friendships among the 277 students. A subset of 21 of these students underwent functional magnetic resonance imaging (fMRI) scans to record brain responses while they watched videos of their classmates. The fMRI participants were later asked to estimate characteristics of these classmates' positions in their shared social network: social distance (degrees of separation between classmates and participants), eigenvector centrality (how well connected a person is to well-connected others), and brokerage (the extent to which classmates bridge different areas of the network). Parkinson reported that the 21 participating students were found to know a great deal about where their classmates were positioned in the network. The researchers then used the fMRI data to investigate whether this network information was retrieved spontaneously in the brain when a participant encountered a familiar classmate. According to Parkinson, it was found that a distinct set of brain regions encoded each of the different network characteristics. Combining these results with knowledge about the functions of the different brain regions, she explained, can provide insight into how particular facets of social networks impact social responses.

Parkinson described another study of brain response and networks in which researchers observed individual differences in how brain regions tracked the popularity of other network members. The relationship between brain activity and the popularity of target group members appeared to be modulated by the perceiver's own popularity, suggesting, she said, "that some people's brains might be more finely tuned to social structure than others." She believes that a useful direction for future research would be to investigate the impact of context and individual differences on how the structure of the social world is processed in the brain.

Parkinson then drew attention to homophily, the notion that people tend to be surrounded by and frequently interact with others who are like themselves in a number of dimensions. Some research on this notion, she said, has focused on coarse variables, such as demographics, to define similarities among people. However, she noted, work in social neuroscience is looking at similarities from the perspective of interpretations of or responses to the world (e.g., similarities in emotions and the allocation of attention). One such study examined the brain responses of a group of people watching the same movie. Over time as the movie continued, Parkinson reported, their brain activity tended to synchronize. The extent to which brain activity aligned across individuals within particular brain regions, she continued, reflected similarities among them in interpretation, memory, and emotional reaction. Parkinson also cited a similar study that examined neural responses to video clips in different dyads among a cohort of graduate students whose social network had been characterized. In this study, the dyads were characterized by the degree of social distance: friends, friends of friends, friends of friends of friends, or dyads who were farther apart in terms of "degrees of separation" in their shared social network. Parkinson reported that this study found greater similarities in neural response among friends than among pairs of people who were farther apart in the social network. She suggested that future research address whether observed similarities in neural processing are a cause or consequence of friendship, and consider the questions of what kinds of similarities predict whether people become friends and the ways in which friends become more similar over time as they associate.

In closing, Parkinson asserted that neuroimaging is a useful research tool because it captures different kinds of processing in parallel and provides a level of information beyond study participants' self-reports. She pointed out that self-reports from study participants may be of limited value because people may be unwilling to share information or unable to provide an accurate account of their thought processes or memories. She argued that combining the tools of neuroscience with methods for characterizing patterns of social relationships would advance research on understanding social cognition and behavior.

THE BRAIN AND SOCIAL NETWORKS

Falk began her presentation by saying she would make the argument that studying brain function within social networks would lead to ways of predicting individual-, group-, and population-level behaviors. To consider how this might work, she provided examples of studies of brain activity in relation to trends in ideas and behaviors. She emphasized that to make progress toward predicting behaviors, it will be necessary for research to consider both the individual and the web of the individual's relationships. She asserted that future research can learn more about the dynamics within social networks by examining individuals (and brains) within the networks and can learn more about brain function by integrating broader contextual information about social network structure and composition with neuroimaging results.

Recent research, Falk noted, has addressed questions about brain activity in individuals receptive to change. Researchers, she said, have found that behavior change is the result of "finding personal value in a new set of ideas or behaviors." She pointed out that a core system in the brain involving the ventromedial prefrontal cortex engages when people make decisions and is part of the brain's "value system." She cited a series of studies that have looked at brain activity, self-reports, and pre/post behaviors of people exposed to persuasive messages about health behaviors ranging from smoking to physical activity to peer influence on risk taking. Researchers, she explained, surveyed participants' attitudes toward such a behavior, their intentions with respect to changing the behavior, and a number of other constructs (e.g., relevant beliefs). In study after study, she reported, brain activity in the value system predicted individual behavior change, explaining variance above and beyond people's self-reports of their intentions and other constructs.

Falk also noted that at the moment people are presented with new information or a new idea, they tend to be vulnerable to discounting it. Initial messages that are confrontational, she elaborated, often elicit defensiveness, whereas specific psychological priming techniques (e.g., value affirmation) reduce the threat of the proposed behavior change and allow a person to perceive greater value in the persuasive messages. She added that studies of brain activity have shown that such use of value affirmation and other priming techniques does increase activity in the brain value system and predict subsequent behavior change.

Falk also pointed out that brain activity has been investigated in small groups of people to examine group behavior in a number of domains, such as information sharing. These studies have observed synchronization in brain activity across members of a group engaged in similar activities (see, for example, findings from group studies previously cited in the summary of Parkinson's presentation). Falk suggested that the value system in the brain of the initial message recipient may be important not only "because it affects individual behavior but it also affects how well a message spreads through a network." She noted that brain activity in the value system of a communicator in response to health news increases the likelihood of sharing, and that preferences spread from communicators' to receivers' brains. Future research, she suggested, could measure brain response to assess the cognition involved in calculating the value of new information. She proposed two questions that may be involved in an individual's decision making: (1) Is this new information relevant to me?, and (2) If other people receive this information, how will sharing it affect my relationships or social status? These types of questions have been studied empirically, she said, and preliminary evidence shows that brain activity significantly predicts the action of sharing information among one's networks.

Falk also noted that social network structure and composition can moderate brain–behavior relationships. To illustrate this point, she provided an example of the effect the type of network surrounding an individual has on decision making. She cited one study that entailed monitoring the behavior and brain activity of about 200 sedentary adults in response to messaging about increasing their physical activity. She reported that people whose friend networks comprised more physically active individuals showed more brain activity in the value system, with corresponding change in behavior involving increased physical activity.

Falk presented another example in which the behavior change among people with different types of social networks was the same, but the underlying brain mechanisms turned out to be different. In this study, she said, participants learned about a mobile phone application and what their peers thought about it, and had to decide whether to recommend it to friends. Participants were classified according to their type of social network—brokerage versus high-closure. She defined brokerage networks as those in which a broker connects people who are otherwise not friends with one another, and hence may be the source of the translation and transmittal of information among network members. A high-closure network, on the other hand, is one in which information flows are confined and shared among network members. According to Falk, the study found no difference in how peer information was ultimately used among participants. However, she said, the study did find differences in brain activity for people with different network structures, suggesting that network association played a role in how brain mechanisms were employed: people with higher levels of information brokerage showed more activation in regions of the brain that have been linked to understanding other people's mental states when deciding what to recommend to peers. She noted that other studies have also demonstrated predictable patterns of brain activity during group interactions that can distinguish participants according to their type of social network.

In closing, Falk argued that future research should continue to examine brain dynamics in relation to social network dynamics and that new multilayer network models are needed to combine these levels of analysis. She proposed some research questions to consider: "Why do ideas spread in some contexts and not others? Who is likely to be most influential in different kinds of social contexts? How can motivation, learning, and performance [be optimized]? How do people learn the structure of their social world? How can . . . optimal interventions [be constructed given] these factors to promote well-being?

EMOTIONAL ARTIFICIAL INTELLIGENCE

Jesse Hoey, University of Waterloo, described his work on developing artificial intelligence (AI) that is capable of operating with groups of human beings on social and emotional levels. Some of the motivation for this work, he said, has come from observing the challenges entailed in collaborations in online networks. He noted that a group of people interacting through and with technology is referred to as a "sociotechnical system."

According to Hoey, the number of people creating online networks for social purposes and collaboration has increased exponentially. He cited the examples of an online community of engineers developing a do-it-yourself autonomous car system and recruiting a network of drivers to help reduce congestion and traffic-related pollution; another group creating apps to aid refugees with migrant issues in Europe; and computer programmers working together virtually to develop new software.[1] He noted that the comments and interactions among people in these online networks can be cordial, but they can also be negative and mean-spirited. To illustrate the challenges of online collaboration, he pointed to the findings of the Open Source Survey, which showed that among the top six reported problems, four could be linked to social and emotional challenges within the network. These challenges included unresponsiveness, dismissive responses, conflict, and unwelcoming language.[2]

A goal of Hoey's research is to build computational models of group behavior in such online teams, or sociotechnical systems. These models, he said, would be used to develop AI agents that could become members of the team, with social, emotional, and cultural grounding "to help change the way that people are behaving on these networks and hopefully make the networks more engaging, more inclusive, and more effective."

Hoey commented on the state of AI. AI, he said, is advanced in some areas, such as computers that can play difficult games and answer complex

---

[1] To find these groups, see https://comma.ai, http://appsforrefugees.com and https://github.com [December 2017].

[2] The survey concluded that "negative interactions are infrequent but highly visible, with consequences for project activity" (see http://opensourcesurvey.org/2017 [December 2017]).

questions and autonomous systems for well-defined tasks. However, he asserted, AI applied to group decision making is much further behind. He illustrated the state of AI with a recent grand challenge to create a team of robots able to play soccer. He pointed out that while these robots can coordinate with each other at a very superficial level, they are nowhere close to what humans can do and lack such features as empathy and altruism that aid decision making in the game. He argued that the robots lacked a model of emotion.

To develop a model of emotion, Hoey has built on pioneering work by Charles Osgood on semantic differential scales.[3] A semantic differential scale, he explained, is a scale with opposing adjectives at each end. To illustrate, he used the concept "polite" with a scale ranging from "rough" to "smooth." Even though polite has little to do with roughness and smoothness, Hoey reported that people sharing the same language and culture will rate polite toward smooth at the same point on the scale with "a remarkable degree of consistency and consensus." This agreement exists, he said, because the terms "feel" the same to people within a culture, and as such, the ratings provide a basis for affective labeling of terms. He added that Osgood's work identified three dimensions that could explain a large percentage of the variance in the data across a number of these semantic scales: (1) evaluation (good to bad), (2) potency (strong to weak), and (3) activity (hyper to sleep).

Hoey suggested that certain fundamental sentiments are implicitly agreed upon. He asserted that when human beings see or enter a social situation, they create "transient impressions" of the people involved, their behaviors, the setting, and so on. These transient impressions can differ from fundamental sentiments, he suggested; however, the tendency is for humans to align their behaviors or emotions so that the situation fits with their fundamental sentiments or such that the situation is emotionally consistent.

Finally, Hoey introduced affect control theory as a mathematical consistency theory that has been operationalized as a computer program.[4] The premise behind affect control theory is that actors in a group behave in ways that cause them to experience transient impressions that are consistent with their fundamental sentiments. The transient impressions and fundamental sentiments are represented mathematically based on the scaling of the three dimensions identified by Osgood. Hoey reported that this theory and the associated computer software are being used in a number of stud-

---

[3] Osgood, C.E. (1952). The nature and measurement of meaning. *Psychological Bulletin*, 49(3), 197–237.
[4] For more information on affect control theory, see Heise, D. (2007). *Expressive Order: Confirming Sentiments in Social Actions*. New York: Springer.

ies to simulate interactions among a group of people and help predict, for example, who might emerge as the leader or who might be excluded. He suggested that as more is learned from this modeling of group interactions, AI can advance to develop artificial agents that may be capable of becoming functional members of human groups.

THE STUDY OF IDENTITIES AND THEIR IMPACT ON NETWORKS

Kenneth Joseph, Northeastern University, began his presentation by emphasizing the importance of social identities in studies of social networks. He highlighted two points: (1) both social identities and social networks have strong and weak versions that combine to affect social behaviors, and (2) both social identities and social networks evolve, and they often evolve together. He defined social identities as "the words and phrases used to label [one's self] and others." His presentation focused on one's own labels of one's self and their effects on behavior. Weak social identities, he said, are situational: they may change as an individual moves from place to place—for example, from home to work. He pointed out that the dichotomy between weak and strong social identities is useful for discussion purposes, but in reality, people's identities fall along a continuum of strength. He added that social identities evolve as individuals learn from their behaviors, as well as those of others. He suggested that data from social media can be a valuable resource for studying identities, and their dynamic nature, within social networks.

Joseph presented an example drawn from recent events to illustrate how strong and weak identities could have played a role in an observed behavior and change in a social network. The example centered on a longtime Buffalo Bills fan who quit his job at the Bills stadium suddenly after members of the team protested the national anthem. Joseph suggested that the fan's connection to the Buffalo Bills fan network, although enduring, was probably a weak part of his social identity. A stronger part of the fan's identity, he said, may have been his identity as a conservative American. In this case, he concluded, a strong identity encouraged a particular behavior that a weak identity, and the weak social ties connected to it, could not prevent.

According to Joseph, this example illustrates the connection between social identity and networks: eliminating part of one's identity resulted in eliminating ties to a particular network. Joseph also emphasized the importance of thinking strategically about the networks being analyzed. He suggested that since people are part of multiple networks, research on the impact of networks on behaviors should consider the strength and stability of the different networks and which might most influence behavior in a given context.

Joseph closed by stating that much remains to be learned about the role of weak and strong identities in behavior. He views social media as an opportunity to observe behavior at scale dynamically over time. For example, with Twitter, people reveal their identities, and they interact in a dynamic social network. Joseph suggested that research look at how particular identities are built and accepted, how identities are used in different networks, how identities are dropped, and how network structures play a role in identity formation.

4

Multilevel, High-Dimensional, Evolving, and Emerging Networks

Noshir Contractor, Northwestern University, a moderator of the panel on this topic, pointed out that the phrase "multilevel, high-dimensional, evolving, and emerging networks" is a descriptive way of characterizing the social networks that have come to be represented by the term "big data." He added that the latter term itself is evolving. Initially, he said, the challenges of big data were referred to as the three V's: volume, velocity, and variety. Now, he explained, researchers have added four more: variability, veracity, visualization, and value. The presentations in this panel examined the advances in and strategies for analysis of networks in which the data involved have these qualities.

EXPLORING DARK NETWORKS

Hsinchun Chen, University of Arizona, addressed the topic of "dark networks," a term that refers to illegal and covert networks. His work on dark networks has encompassed gang and narcotic networks, extremist and terrorist networks, and computer hackers. He noted that he has examined these networks from a data science perspective, drawing on data and text mining and visualization tools, particularly in a multilingual context.

Chen's initial work in this area led to the development of a crime information-sharing and data mining tool known as COPLINK. He explained that this tool draws on millions of records from multiple databases containing both some structured data, such as those from police reports, and unstructured data. He pointed out that even with structured data, false identities are possible. Accordingly, he said, instead of relying on single points of information, the tool draws inferences from relations and multiple reports of similar relations, and not just among people but also between people and locations, vehicles, dates, and so on.

Chen provided the example of an application used in border crossing situations, which he characterized as a high-risk vehicle identification system. The system, he said, collects cross-jurisdictional information from multiple databases. A license plate reader captures a vehicle's license plate information and within seconds, the data mining tool generates associations between the license plate and other types of information, such as the vehicle's owner and other Department of Motor Vehicles information, police records, and the context of the crossing (e.g., day, time, other vehicles). From these associations or the absence of associations, Chen explained, the tool predicts whether a particular vehicle crossing is benign or at high risk of narcotic activity.

Chen noted that similar data mining techniques have been used in another project to examine terrorist networks and recruiting efforts through social media. In this case, the amount of information is vast (terabytes), but the challenge is that it resides on the dark web, a term referring to Internet sites that cannot be accessed by standard search engines, are encrypted, and can be accessed only by special software. According to Chen, this situation represents a different type of data collection in which all the available information must be collected at once and then stored prior to analysis. He explained that the analysis of these online communications draws on linguistic theories. The project, he elaborated, developed writing signatures for different authors, or "writeprints" (akin to fingerprints), that make it possible to follow an author across different forums even if the person uses different screen names. Chen added that developing these signatures was not an easy task given that writing features (e.g., syntactic and lexical features) had to be analyzed for multiple languages, including Arabic, English, French, German, and Russian. Once the signatures had been developed, he explained, authors with similar messages were identified, and a model of relationships was created. According to Chen, the analysis and tools resulting from this project proved useful for identifying members of terrorist networks who were overt—for example, already appearing on police records for some reason. "Smarter" members, he said, could not be identified by computer analysis alone; human insight was needed.

Chen's data techniques were applied more recently to cybersecurity issues (e.g., computer hackers stealing credit card information). In this project, he explained, the object is not only to identify the hackers but also to identify the product or source code involved. But even when searching for computer codes, he said, the process of drawing associations and linking features is important to identifying high-risk subjects. He noted that people who specialize in bank exploits also specialize in cryptology that can be used in ransomware. He added that this project has developed tools with which to search the dark web and online forums for exploitive source codes, tutorials on creating malicious documents, and malware attachments. The malware attachments, he said, indicate the expertise that was needed to create the malware, pointing to particular specialists.

In closing, Chen listed several challenges in using social network analysis for practical purposes, including identifying appropriate data sources (a great deal of open-source information is available on the Internet, but not all of it will be useful); recognizing appropriate nodes and levels as well as appropriate entities to extract (e.g., identities, writeprints); establishing appropriate links (e.g., linked by associations, time and space, or conversations); and tracking changes over time. He proposed that researchers continue to develop tools and methodological foundations for better understanding dark networks, hidden networks, noise, deception, and adversarial intents. He suggested further that advanced tools could improve the comprehensive and timely collection of open-source information; that AI could assist with entity and relationship recognition; and that advanced data analytics could expand research opportunities. Finally, he cited research on adversarial machine learning[1] as an area potentially poised for advancement.

ROBUST SUMMARY STATISTICS FOR NETWORKS

Benjamin Golub, Harvard University, gave an overview of some of the research questions often asked about networks and their processes. He also made an argument for simple, physics-inspired models and greater interdisciplinary work going forward.

The kinds of networks Golub considers are groups of agents involved in decision making, whether it involves productive or adversarial decisions. When thinking about group decision making, he explained, several natural questions arise: Who are the most influential agents in a network? Is a network good at coordinating? How can a network be disrupted (i.e., what interventions work)? He characterized these as scientific questions that can be investigated for different types of groups or networks, from high school students to terrorist organizations.

Work in economics and related fields, Golub continued, has provided insights into these questions. For determining who is influential, he suggested network science has focused on the concept of centrality, particularly eigenvector measures. For determining how well a group coordinates, he said, the field has focused on features of homophily, cohesion, and segrega-

---

[1] Adversarial machine learning involves investigating ways to incorporate machine learning techniques safely in adversarial settings such as spam filtering and malware detection.

tion. He stated that a rich spectrum of mathematical techniques are available with which to measure these features. With regard to interventions to influence group decision making, he noted there are some studies, but the literature is not robust.

Golub suggested that until more is known about how networks respond to interventions, it is difficult to operationalize the theories behind networks. He listed some of the practical complications involved in conducting research on networks. The first is that networks are adaptive and dynamic and respond to interventions in ways that change the networks' very nature. Golub offered the example of research on drug trafficking that demonstrated the response of trafficking networks to enforcement measures.[2] He added that game theoretic modeling, which takes into account agents who are aware of interventions, has application to adaptive networks.

Golub cited as a second complication that networks are not perfectly observed, for two reasons: (1) random noise, and (2) nonrandom error that results because certain relationships may not be activated. In the latter case, he explained that the activation of relationships within a network is highly dependent on context, so that key relationships may not be activated at the time when data on the network are collected. For example, he said, people do not seek advice all the time even if they have access to a friend who can provide it. In addition, for certain events, some relationships or links will not be activated until the day of the event. Golub characterized this as a fairly standard error, a problem even in mundane contexts and not confined to events considered by the Intelligence Community. He added that econometricians have developed methods with which to adjust for this error in statistical estimation.

The final complication cited by Golub was computational costs. Even if enough resources, time, and energy were available to collect massive amounts of information on a network, he explained, the computational power and time needed to run the statistical analyses of this information would be impractical. Thus there are good reasons, he said, to measure only parts of a network.

Golub then turned to the use of models, noting that good models can aid understanding even when only part of a network can be measured. He suggested that the best models with significant scientific impact are "simple, physics-inspired" ones in which intuiting physical or social forces helps in envisioning how a network or system is working. Bad models, on the other hand, are highly combinatorial and algorithmic, and often entail black box operations in which the applied theory of social process is unclear. Golub suggested a focus on useful decompositions as a way to develop success-

---

[2] Dell, M. (2015). Trafficking networks and the Mexican drug war. *American Economic Review*, *105*(6), 1738–1779.

ful models, using the analogy of a drum to explain decompositions. The motion of a drum, he said, can be decomposed into characteristic modes or principal oscillations. Any impulse to the drum can be decomposed to these component pieces, which in turn can be understood as contributing to the drum's vibration. Golub suggested that the same mathematics and decomposition techniques can be applied to networks. Once the important components have been identified through decomposition, he added, it is important to find easy ways to measure these components.

According to Golub, what is needed in the future is the development of robust statistical models of individual network components. This can be accomplished, he argued, by training people and creating more interdisciplinary research teams at the intersection of game theory, physics, and statistics. He elaborated that those with expertise in game theory and physics can help build models that incorporate reasonable decision making and laws of motion and decomposition, while those with statistical expertise can ensure that the models are robust to sampling and account for systematic bias in the network links.

In closing, Golub reiterated that much can be understood about networks, their processes, and their response to interventions without extensive data collection. It is efficient and meaningful, he asserted, to measure just a part of a network—the part determined to be affected by interventions of interest. Expanding on this thought, he offered the analogy of functional magnetic resonance imaging experiments and suggested that useful science will test interventions so as to "shine something at the system [or network] and see how it vibrates."

THE FUTURE OF COMPLEX NETWORKS

Alexander Volfovsky, Duke University, spoke about the challenges of using statistical techniques to study causal relationships within networks. He briefly considered a network of people, modeling approaches, and the types of experiments that would be run on such a network. Volfovsky suggested that the different nodes could represent different attributes of people, and a model could be created to explain what types of attributes link people together as friends. Once such a model has been created, he said, it can be used to predict the friendship links that will develop when a new person enters the network or reactions within the network when a certain treatment is applied to the model.

Volfovsky reported that researchers often cluster the people or nodes in a network into groups or communities in some way to detect something of interest inside the network. He discussed some of the challenges of detecting these communities. First, communities are frequently based on more than one attribute. Volfovsky explained that simple models, such as the stochastic block model, may not account for more than one attribute, and that adding complexity to these models just increases the computational time, which at some point becomes impractical. He cited spectral methods as a simpler approach that would yield the same or approximately the same results. However, he asserted, even these methods are limited in scalability. He argued that new tools are needed to address very large networks.

Describing a second challenge, Volfovsky pointed out that communities are more difficult to detect as they become more interconnected. He noted that algorithms exist for detecting communities with no or weak interconnections, but that current algorithms have difficulty detecting communities when strong connections exist among people in different communities. He noted there are some models for such situations, but they are computationally extensive.

Volfovsky described a study using data from the National Longitudinal Study of Adolescent to Adult Health (AddHealth) to illustrate the limitations of simple models and the need for developing models that directly account for the data collection process. As part of the AddHealth study, American high school students were asked to identify their top five friends. Volfovsky and colleagues used the resulting dataset to connect network characteristics to individual behavior, that is, to understand factors contributing to friendships and whether such relationships could be predicted. Volfovsky explained that the use of latent variable models is the standard in statistics for this type of investigation. However, he added, a number of assumptions are made in using these models, one of which is that the data reflect correct observations: in other words, the models do not account for the possibility that the data may be ranked or in some way censored. He noted that the AddHealth survey did indeed censor some data by limiting respondents to five friends (i.e., students with five or fewer friends had their friends recorded, whereas the data on students with more than five friends were limited). Volfovsky and colleagues incorporated this information on how the data were collected into their model of network characteristics and friendships, introducing a likelihood that accommodated the ranked and censored nature of the data and allowed for unbiased estimation of regression effects. Their model was able to predict how many friends a person would have if allowed to name as many friends as desired.

Volfovsky noted that this type of modeling can also assist in developing an understanding of causality within networks by informing the development of better experiments. Such experiments, according to Volfovsky, are currently the best techniques for examining causal relationships within a network. He argued that research advances in this area would require determining how to combine observational data with the experimental results. He pointed to the body of literature in metrics and statistics on drawing causal inferences from observational and experimental data, but for much simpler contexts, and suggested that researchers need to build on this work to expand statistical techniques for applicability to complex network structures.

Volfovsky cited the example of an effort to understand the efficacy of isolation as treatment for influenza-like illnesses. He argued that the classic approach of subtracting the average outcome for controls from the average outcome for the treated was limited. New tools are emerging, he said, with which to estimate causal effects in networks, which is a substantially more difficult problem since networks likely influence both the outcomes and the way in which the outcomes are observed.

In closing, Volfovsky suggested three areas that need to be addressed in the near future: substantive network challenges (i.e., better understanding of positions, relationships, and trigger points in a network); statistical techniques for addressing uncertainties in observed networks; and engineering solutions to the current computational expense of available models.

5

Discussion

This chapter summarizes some of the discussion among presenters and other participants throughout the workshop. Among the many points raised and questions asked of presenters, this summary focuses on those aspects of the discussion relevant to the purpose of this workshop, as articulated in Chapter 1: to gather information for the Decadal Survey of relevance to the Intelligence Community (IC) on emerging trends and future directions in the research area of social network thinking.[1]

COLLABORATION NETWORKS IN THE IC

Randolph H. Pherson, Pherson Associates, was asked to provide his perspective on the relevance of the presented research programs and ideas to the IC. As a consultant to the IC, he has had considerable experience working in teams and forming professional networks (or what he prefers to call "collaborative communities") across agencies within the IC. He noted that all agencies within the IC have made considerable efforts to examine existing collaborative communities that appeared to work well and create new communities incorporating their features.

Pherson pointed out that some of the most effective communities were found to be those that drew their members from those who had worked together before; they could form a cohesive group quickly. Having members with networking skills that translated to connections with people and

---

[1] For an archive of the full workshop Webcast, including discussion sessions, see http://sites.nationalacademies.org/DBASSE/BBCSS/DBASSE_181267 [December 2017].

resources outside the community was also helpful. He said he had found that communities that struggled to work together efficiently lacked mutual trust and had miscommunication problems, often as a result of being too large or too entangled in bureaucratic matters.

Pherson listed six imperatives he regards as necessary for professional networks to ensure effective collaboration and information sharing: (1) mutual trust, (2) mutual benefit, (3) incentives, (4) mission criticality, (5) access and agility, and (6) a common lexicon. He elaborated that for these communities, mutual trust refers to a willingness to demonstrate one's own vulnerability; mutual benefit refers to everyone getting something productive out of the effort; incentives refer to support from management and leadership to engage in collaborative behaviors; mission criticality refers to recognition that collaboration should revolve around what team members must do every day and not be considered an add-on task; access and agility refer to permission and flexibility to participate; and a common lexicon refers to having common understandings of language, definitions, and rules of operation.

AREAS FOR FURTHER RESEARCH ON NETWORKS AND NETWORK THINKING

Pherson identified several areas in which further research on networks and network thinking could help inform the IC's collaborative communities and their analysis of security issues. He suggested that more research could be conducted on the issue of trust within teams—how to build it and use it to bolster collaboration, as well as integrate new people into an existing team. He also highlighted the potential for research to address the challenges of information processing by developing tools to manage and help critically analyze the large amounts of information available, including the identification of any misinformation and information gaps.

Pherson expressed his view that the workshop presentations had focused attention on analytic areas worth the IC's consideration, given that the future presents a different set of security problems than have been considered in the past. For example, he pointed to the applicability of the science of urban networks to models of political instability, as well as to humanitarian crises (e.g., current migration issues in Europe). He also suggested that the neuroscience work presented at the workshop would help clarify how like-minded networks develop, and could also enhance understanding of brain functions and subsequent behaviors in different contexts, such as when network interactions and communications take place in person compared with virtually. He speculated further that the concept of social identities presented by Kenneth Joseph could be applicable to deradicalization theories.

Kathleen Carley, Carnegie Mellon University, asked all the presenters to identify future research investments most likely to advance the science of social networks and social network thinking over the next 10 years and ensure its relevance and usefulness to the IC.

Regina Joseph, New York University, reinforced the importance of research on building trust within teams. She also suggested the need for research on identifying people with the right analytic skills and diversity of expertise to contribute to analytic teams within the IC in the evolving information environment.

Guido Cervone, Pennsylvania State University, asserted that research on human–machine interactions will be critical. He argued that since both the capability of the analyst and the output of automated decision-making algorithms are limited, efforts should focus on ways to combine the intuition of experienced analysts with machine outputs. He suggested that systems and professional networks be developed to take advantage of knowledge in different forms. This would require integrating the experience and knowledge of people possessing structured information from official data collections with the output of information generated by automated data mining systems.

Cervone commented on emerging technologies and their potential impact on research. He highlighted the increasing use of large combined datasets that include different types of data from such sources as remote sensing, numerical models, and social media. He also pointed out that although Cloud storage is nearly unlimited, data are accumulating at a much faster pace than the rate at which the data can be transferred to the Cloud and analyzed. The current trend in research, he said, is edge computing, whereby some of the research computation is carried out where the data initially reside. He mentioned two other technological advances: high-performance computing (e.g., exascale computing) and the ability to collect data in real time with one's smartphone.

Jesse Hoey, University of Waterloo, pointed out that work in artificial intelligence is heavily data-driven. He argued for greater emphasis on building social or cultural models from such disciplines as sociology, psychology, and cognitive science to inform artificial intelligence systems. Kenneth Joseph, Northeastern University, expressed concern that some machine-learning approaches are starting to emulate human cognitive biases. He suggested that research explore how cognitive biases come to be embedded in data, how algorithms learn them, how this affects outputs from automated systems, and whether embedded biases in data can be leveraged by adversaries.

Markus Mobius, Microsoft Research, pointed out that little is known about individuals' processing of communication and aggregation of information to take particular positions. He noted that while research can measure outcomes and behavior, little is known about the internal processes involved. He drew attention to the longer life cycle of information and misinformation today relative to the past (i.e., people used to consume information in a newspaper in a day, whereas information now lives on for much longer in digital media). He also noted that in the current social media environment, information can appear as though it comes from multiple sources when it may in fact be from a single source.

Carolyn Parkinson, University of California, Los Angeles, said there has been some research on the structure of networks and the identification of network opportunities for communication. She suggested that future research investigate how different network structures impact information sharing and how a particular structure may impact the weight assigned to information or network members' receptiveness to misinformation. She also suggested that research could be designed to examine people's identification of a source of information, as well as their knowledge of that source and its relation to other sources, and how that source identification sways their positions or behaviors. In addition, she said, research could investigate how different people in structurally different network positions use their brains differently. Findings from this line of inquiry, she noted, could have consequences for identifying those who are more effectively targeted or influenced in certain situations. However, she cautioned, to understand individual differences using neuroscience techniques, a larger sample size is needed than that typically used for cognitive neuroscience experiments. She emphasized the promise of funding efforts that would bring together complementary expertise and create research teams able to integrate knowledge from psychology, cognitive neuroscience, sociology, social network thinking, and statistics.

Both Emily Falk, University of Pennsylvania, and Zachary Neal, Michigan State University, agreed that interdisciplinary teams will be important in the future. In response to a question on whether brain activity for decision making works the same way when messages are ill-intended (i.e., designed to get people to do something wrong instead of encouraging positive behaviors), Falk acknowledged that her work has focused on health-related behaviors and that neuroscience research on decision making in adults has generally focused on prohealth or prosocial choices. However, she noted, a large literature exists on risky decision making, particularly in teens and clinical populations. She suggested that research combining neuroscience and social network thinking could be expanded to consider brain functioning in decision making in response to ill-intended messaging. Neal, drawing on his experience in the field of urban networks, said he believes the research is tackling the right questions (e.g., Where do people, ideas, and money reside, and how are they connected? How and where do they move?). New questions are not needed, he asserted, but merging talent across disciplines would enable the field to do a better job of answering existing questions. He highlighted as a challenge that each discipline brings its own specialization and language, such that researchers from different disciplines may be talking about the same thing without that being clear (e.g., the social sciences use the terms "nodes" and "edges," while mathematics refers to "vertices").

Hsinchun Chen, University of Arizona, suggested a different approach to the importance of interdisciplinary work—what he called a "three-leg approach to human data fusion." In developing data mining tools for practical applications, he found that this work requires knowledge from the social and behavioral sciences to provide theory and explanations for social behaviors; analytic techniques from the data sciences to enable the aggregation of information from noisy data; and input from practitioners to provide insight on application and practical challenges. He emphasized that these three elements all need to be present to operationalize applications that involve data on human behavior and communications. He added that he sees more collaboration today than when he started in this area of research 20 years ago.

Benjamin Golub, Harvard University, called attention to research laboratories within commercial companies such as Microsoft. These labs, he said, follow a common approach of letting bright scholars work together in pursuing academic studies of interest to them within the companies' domains of work. According to Golub, the studies are often innovative, and eventually companies can leverage some of the findings they yield.

DATA NEEDS

A number of workshop participants pointed out that a large portion of social media data is controlled by private companies. Golub argued that a good, open data resource is needed for academics. Alexander Volfovsky, Duke University, agreed and asserted that no useful and easily accessible data are available with which to validate models. Chen noted that some longitudinal social media datasets are becoming available to social scientists and data scientists, although the data often lack identifying labels. Noshir Contractor, Northwestern University, added that some data that have been acquired from companies were not collected for research purposes but often come from server logs and were collected to help software engineers debug their platforms.

Contractor asked whether it would be possible to reengineer these platforms to collect data that would be more useful to researchers, and whether an agreement could be formulated that would allow the research community more regular access to social media data, sufficiently anonymized but still useful and labeled in some way. Volfovsky argued that it may be more efficient to use by-product data than to create completely new pathways for data creation. He suggested gaining a better understanding of how and why the data are generated and embedding that knowledge in research models. On the other hand, he pointed to current experimentation on platforms that may collect the type of data useful for answering research questions. He also suggested that reaching agreement with companies for regular use of their data is unlikely because of the risk of research findings being misinterpreted and damaging to companies.

Golub asserted that any new set of data should be a "living" resource and not just a better dataset. He elaborated that regardless of how well a data collection is designed, researchers will continue to investigate different questions that will require different types of data in the future.

Marcus Mobius, Microsoft, noted that much of the data collected by companies has a short life. He highlighted data retention rules and legal requirements, especially in the European Union, that require companies to dispose of personal data after a certain period of time. He proposed developing anonymized, summary statistics to create a historical record of social activity without violating data retention rules. He acknowledged that some form of a consensus process would be necessary among the various research communities to determine how these summary statistics would be created and what information they would include. He pointed to Google Trends as an example of a successful statistical summary, one that has been used in many research papers. He proposed that an investment be made in developing more summary statistics for research instead of trying to determine how to transfer large amounts of data.

ETHICAL CONSIDERATIONS IN CONDUCTING RESEARCH ON SOCIAL NETWORKS

Scott Feld, Purdue University, offered two purposes for the research discussed at the workshop. The first, he said, is to understand networks in order to improve networks and build networks that effectively make progress toward goals. He offered the example of developing better teams in the IC to share and use intelligence information more effectively. A second purpose, he continued, is to understand how networks operate (e.g., how relationships develop and information spreads) in order to predict, control, or possibly disrupt behaviors.

Feld was asked to reflect on the ethics of conducting research on social networks. He defined ethics as "doing [one's] work in an appropriate and socially acceptable way." He explained that ethical concerns fall into three categories: (1) human subjects, (2) institution of science, and (3) responsibilities to the broader community and society. He stated that it is appropriate to worry about and protect from harm both people who are direct participants in research studies (through informed consent and human subject approvals) and those whose personal information becomes part of studies, whether with their permission or covertly. He noted that researchers also have responsibility to their institutions and the institution of science, adding that they are expected to provide useful information, new knowledge, and generalizable results in exchange for infrastructure and funding.

Feld continued by asserting that research intended to inform the work of the IC or government must be undertaken with a well-defined understanding of that work. What this means, he said, is that data should be collected and theories considered that are relevant to the specific context at hand. He encouraged researchers to be humble and honest about what is known, what is not known, and any limitations of their research findings. It is important, he said, to think about what could be wrong with findings and why.

Feld raised a final ethical concern related to the effects on the community or society. He noted that research is often pursued for the public good, in an attempt to find optimal solutions to societal problems. For contexts involving an adversary, however, he raised the dilemma of the potential use of expertise to develop knowledge that may "cause harm in the interest of causing good." He offered no easy solution to this dilemma, but emphasized the importance of considering the potential consequences of developing capabilities, knowledge, and sources of information that may impact society in negative ways.

CLOSING

Contractor and Carley closed the workshop by presenting their takeaways from the workshop presentations and discussions. Contractor focused on the tension between data-driven and theory-driven approaches to modeling. He underscored the importance of work on causal inference, which he characterized as an important methodological issue for moving the field of network science beyond describing networks to evaluating their processes and outcomes. He added that the type of research envisioned at the workshop will require interdisciplinary teams whose members have enough knowledge of each other's areas of expertise to engage collectively in solving some of the research challenges highlighted at the workshop.

Carley commented that network science, much like statistics, is being projected to become part of every discipline, and the workshop had demonstrated the truth of this projection. She observed that the workshop had included much discussion of network metrics and the large amount of data available, but little discussion on interpreting and manipulating networks. She emphasized that although the amount of data has grown, the data are still biased and incomplete, and she asserted that new tools for analysis are needed to address the uncertainties that result. She noted that the issue of cognitive bias had been mentioned; however, she called attention to the notion of stylized facts or known network biases. She suggested that scholars in the field of network science think about creating anthologies of robust findings in this area to help the IC and new researchers recognize what is implicit in the science of network thinking.

Appendix A

Statement of Task for the Decadal Survey of Social and Behavioral Sciences for Applications to National Security

The National Academies of Sciences, Engineering, and Medicine will carry out a decadal survey on the social and behavioral sciences (SBS) in areas relevant to national security in two integrated phases. The first phase, a national summit (workshop), was completed in fall 2016. The statement of task for the second phase, a consensus process, is below.

An ad hoc consensus committee, drawing on membership from the summit steering committee, will be appointed to conduct the decadal survey aimed at identifying opportunities that are poised to contribute significantly to the Intelligence Community's (IC's) analytic responsibilities. The study will identify opportunities throughout the social sciences (e.g., sociology, demography, political science, economics, and anthropology) and from behavioral sciences (e.g., psychology, cognition, and neuroscience) and will draw on discussions at the summit to frame its inquiry. Attention will also be paid to work in allied professional disciplines such as engineering, business, and law, and a full variety of cross-disciplinary, historical, case study, participant, and phronetic approaches.

The committee will work with the Office of the Director of National Intelligence (ODNI) and security community members to understand government needs and expectations. The final report will be based on the committee's consideration of broad national security priorities; relevant capabilities of elements within the security community to support and apply SBS research findings; cost and technical readiness; likely growth of research programs; emerging SBS data, procedures, personnel, and other resources; and opportunities to leverage related research activities not directly supported by government. The committee will specify a range of relevant work that could be useful to the IC for their consideration in developing future research priorities.

The committee's primary tasks will be to:

1. Assess progress in addressing selected major social and behavioral scientific challenges that might prove useful to national security. Include discussion of approaches that are gaining strength and those that are losing strength.
2. Identify SBS opportunities that can be used to guide security-community investment decisions and application efforts over the next 10 years.
3. Specify approaches to facilitate productive interchange between the security community and the external social science research community.
4. Reflect on the application of the decadal model to the SBS and identify lessons learned (insights into how to approach and perform the decadal survey process) and promising practices (activities that could facilitate future decadal surveys in the SBS and similar disciplines and maximize their ultimate utilities to sponsors and the scientific community).

Appendix B

Workshop Agenda

LEVERAGING ADVANCES IN SOCIAL NETWORK THINKING FOR NATIONAL SECURITY: A WORKSHOP
October 11, 2017

Keck Center
500 Fifth Street, NW
Washington, DC
Room 201

8:30 a.m.	Workshop Registration Opens
9:00 a.m.	Workshop Commence

9:00 a.m.	**Welcome and Overview of Events**
	Sujeeta Bhatt, Study Director
	    Audience information
	Paul Sackett, University of Minnesota, SBS Decadal Survey Chair
	    Welcome
	David Honey, Director of Science and Technology, ODNI, Study Sponsor
	    Sponsor perspective and context for study and workshops

9:30 a.m.	**Opening Remarks on the Future of Social Network Thinking** Kathleen Carley, Carnegie Mellon University, Workshop Committee Chair

Research Panel Presentations and Discussion

9:45 a.m.   Panel 1: Networks-Plus—Beyond the Individual

This panel will consider advances in combining social network thinking with new types of data. Research in this area will have an external focus on the position of individuals in the social and physical world. Key questions are as follows: What are the gains to be made from a multilevel network analysis approach? How is a social network science embedded in the physical world valuable from an Intelligence Community perspective? Where could major gains be made with a small investment in research?

Moderators: Kathleen Carley, Carnegie Mellon University, and Matthew Brashears, University of South Carolina

Leslie DeChurch, Northwestern University
    Title: Organizing in Teams
Zachary Neal, Michigan State University
    Title: The Future of Urban Network Research
Regina Joseph, New York University
    Title: Supersynthesizers: Confronting the Coming Analytical Crisis in an Age of Influence
Guido Cervone, Pennsylvania State University
    Title: Use of Crowdsourced Data During Emergencies

10:35 a.m.   Response to Presentations
Randolph H. Pherson, Pherson Associates, LLC

10:45 a.m.   Discussion and Q&A
Moderators, Presenters, and Members of the Committee on a Decadal Survey of Social and Behavioral Sciences for Applications to National Security

11:45 a.m.   **LUNCH**

12:45 p.m.   Panel 2: Networks-Plus—Within the Individual

This panel will consider advances in combining social network thinking with new types of investigations on cognition, neural influences, and social psychology. Research in this area will have an internal focus on how individuals perceive and process the social and physical world. Key questions are as follows: What are the gains to be made by bringing cognition, perception, affect, and an understanding of the actor's identity into social network modeling? How is a "cognitive" network science useful from an Intelligence Community perspective? Where could major gains be made with a small investment in research?

Moderators: Noshir Contractor, Northwestern University, and Emily Falk, University of Pennsylvania

Carolyn Parkinson, University of California, Los Angeles
   Title: The Brain in the Social World: Integrating Approaches from Social Neuroscience, Psychology, and Social Network Analysis
Emily Falk, University of Pennsylvania (virtual presenter)
   Title: Brain and Social Networks: Fundamental Building Blocks of Human Experience
Jesse Hoey, University of Waterloo
   Title: Emotional Artificial Intelligence in Sociotechnical Systems
Kenneth Joseph, Northeastern University
   Title: Studying Identities and Their Impact on Networks Using Social Media Data

1:35 p.m.   **Response to Presentations**
Randolph H. Pherson, Pherson Associates, LLC

1:45 p.m.   **Discussion and Q&A**
Moderators, Presenters, and Members of the Committee on a Decadal Survey of Social and Behavioral Sciences for Applications to National Security

2:30 p.m.   **BREAK**

2:45 p.m.	**Panel 3: Multilevel, High-Dimensional, Evolving, and Emerging Networks**

This panel will consider advances in understanding networks that take into account the dynamic nature of networks and core challenges that impact certainty, such as data bias, data stationarity, and hidden data. Key questions are as follows: How are advances in this area useful from an Intelligence Community perspective? Where could major gains be made with a small investment in research? What are the core challenges for social network analysis when dealing with large datasets where the data may be partially hidden or covert and the sampled network itself may be random, evolving, or stationary?

Moderators: Noshir Contractor, Northwestern University, and Markus Mobius, Microsoft

Hsinchun Chen, University of Arizona
    Title: *Exploring Dark Networks: From the Surface Web to the Dark Web*
Benjamin Golub, Harvard University
    Title: *Robust Summary Statistics for Strategic and Social Processes in Networks*
Alexander Volfovsky, Duke University
    Title: *The Future of Complex Networks: Statistics, Algorithms, and Causality* |
| 3:35 p.m. | **Response to Presentations**
Randolph H. Pherson, Pherson Associates, LLC |
| 3:45 p.m. | **Discussion and Q&A**
Moderators, Presenters, and Members of the Committee on a Decadal Survey of Social and Behavioral Sciences for Applications to National Security |
| 4:30 p.m. | **Summative Comments**
Scott Feld, Purdue University |
| 4:50 p.m. | **Closing Remarks**
Kathleen Carley, Carnegie Mellon University, Workshop Committee Chair |
| 5:00 p.m. | **ADJOURN** |

Appendix C

Participants List

Listed here are the individuals who attended one or more of three workshops held October 11, 2017, to gather information for the Decadal Survey of Social and Behavioral Sciences for Applications to National Security.

Vincent Alcazar
Vincent Alcazar, LLC

Alexandra Beatty
National Academies

Andrew Bennett
Georgetown University

Gary G. Berntson
Ohio State University

Sujeeta Bhatt
National Academies

Jordan A. Blenner
Lewis-Burke Associates, LLC

Matthew Brashears
University of South Carolina

Christa Brelsford
Oak Ridge National Laboratory

David Broniatowski
George Washington University

Dennis Buede
Innovative Decisions, Inc.

Rita Bush
National Security Agency

Kathleen Carley
Carnegie Mellon University

Lina Cepeda
United Nations

Guido Cervone
Pennsylvania State University

Hsinchun Chen
University of Arizona

Richard Cincotta
Stimson Center

Kyle Clark
U.S. Department of Homeland
  Security

Noshir Contractor
Northwestern University

Bradley Cooke
National Science Foundation

Chris Cox
Defense Intelligence Agency

Thelma Cox
National Academies

Skyler Cranmer
Ohio State University

Bruce Crawford
Independent Researcher

Leslie DeChurch
Northwestern University

Daniel Demus
Defense Threat Reduction Agency

David Dornisch
U.S. Government Accountability
  Office

Barbara Anne Dosher
University of California, Irvine

Jennifer Dresden
Georgetown University

William Dressler
University of Alabama

Anna Duran
Avatar Research Institute

Jesse A. Egbert
Northern Arizona University

Kacey Ernst
Arizona University

Emily Falk
University of Pennsylvania

Scott Feld
Purdue University

Suzanne Fry
National Intelligence Council

George G.
U.S. Government

Sumit Ganguly
Indiana University

Michele Gelfand
University of Maryland

Christopher Gelpi
Ohio State University

James Goldgeier
American University

APPENDIX C

Benjamin Golub
Harvard University

Hal Greenwald
MITRE

Winston Harris
Defense Threat Reduction Agency

Richard Harknett
University of Cincinnati

Jesse Hoey
University of Waterloo

Michael Holtje
U.S. Department of Treasury

David Honey
Office of the Director of National Intelligence

John Hoven
Independent Consultant

Judith Jacobson
Innovative Decisions, Inc.

Gary Jin
U.S. Department of Homeland Security

Jeffrey C. Johnson
University of Florida

Kenneth Joseph
Northeastern University

Regina Joseph
New York University

Dan Kahan
Yale University

Sallie Keller
Virginia Polytechnic Institute and State University

Jacklyn Kerr
Stanford University

Giuseppe (Joe) Labianca
University of Kentucky

Deborah Larson
University of California, Los Angeles

Mark Liberman
University of Pennsylvania

Herb Lin
Stanford University

Sean Lynn-Jones
Harvard University

Anthony Mann
National Academies

David Matsumoto
San Francisco State University

Shana McLean
IARPA

Carmen Medina
MedinAnalytics, LLC

Asma Melebrai
Government Contractor

Katherine Meyer
National Science Foundation

Marc Dean Millot
Good Harbor Partners

Mahmoud Moamenah
Government Contractor

Markus Mobius
Microsoft Research

Fran P. Moore
FPM Consulting, LLC

Amanda Murdie
University of Georgia

Dhiraj Murthy
University of Texas

Kent Myers
Office of the Director of National Intelligence

Zachary Neal
Michigan State University

Howard C. Nusbaum
National Science Foundation

Robert O'Connor
National Science Foundation

Nedim Ogelman
U.S. Department of State

Carolyn Parkinson
University of California, Los Angeles

Randolph H. Pherson
Pherson Associates, LLC

Jennarose Placitella
University of Pennsylvania

Ted Plasse
U.S. Department of Defense

Alyson Reed
Linguistic Society of America

Philip Resnik
University of Maryland

Joy Rohde
University of Michigan

Benjamin Ryan
Gallup, Inc.

Paul R. Sackett
University of Minnesota

Laura Sappelsa
ANSER

Julie Schuck
National Academies

Afreen Siddiqi
Massachusetts Institute of Technology

Michael Siri
National Academies

Robert Smith
University of Maryland

Laura Steckman
MITRE

Anita Street
Office of the Director of National Intelligence

Jim Sullivan
Central Intelligence Agency

Gwyneth Sutherlin
Geographic Services, Inc.

Jeffrey Taliaferro
Tufts University

Steve Thompson
Office of the Director of National Intelligence

William R. Thompson
Indiana University

Elizabeth Townsend
National Academies

Lisa Troyer
Army Research Office

Garrett Tyson
National Academies

Stuart Umpleby
George Washington University

Alexander Volfovsky
Duke University

Kate Von Holle
University of Chicago

Barbara Wanchisen
National Academies

Steven Ward
Cornell University

Susan Weller
University of Texas

Mitzi Wertheim
Naval Postgraduate School

Renée L. Wilson Gaines
National Academies

Jeremy Wolfe
Brigham & Women's Hospital, Harvard Medical School

Mary Zalesny
Defense Threat Reduction Agency

Appendix D

Biographical Sketches of Steering Committee Members and Presenters

Sujeeta Bhatt (*Study Director*) is a senior program officer with the National Academies of Sciences, Engineering, and Medicine and study director for the Decadal Survey of Social and Behavioral Sciences for Applications to National Security. She was formerly a research scientist at the Defense Intelligence Agency (DIA) and was detailed to the Federal Bureau of Investigation's High-Value Detainee Interrogation Group (HIG). Prior to that, she was an assistant professor in the Department of Radiology at the Georgetown University Medical Center on detail to DIA/HIG. Her work at DIA and HIG entailed identifying knowledge gaps and developing and managing research projects to address those gaps. Her work in the Intelligence Community focused on the psychological and neuroscience bases for credibility assessment, biometrics, insider threat, intelligence interviewing and interrogation methods, and the development of research-to-practice modules on interrogation-related topics to promote the use of evidence-based practice in interviews/interrogations. She holds a Ph.D. in behavioral neuroscience from American University.

Matthew E. Brashears (*Committee Member*) is an associate professor of sociology at the University of South Carolina. His work crosses levels, integrating ideas from evolutionary theory, social networks, organizational theory, and neuroscience. His current research focuses on linking cognition to social network structure, studying the effects of error and error correction on diffusion dynamics, and using ecological models to connect individual behavior to collective dynamics. He is also engaged in an effort to model values and interactional scripts in an ecological space using cross-national data, with the goal of generating a predictive model of cultural competition and evolution. He earned his Ph.D. in sociology from the University of Arizona.

Kathleen Carley (*Committee Chair*) is a professor of computer science in the Institute for Software Research and director of the Center for Computational Analysis of Social and Organizational Systems at Carnegie Mellon University. She is also CEO of Carley Technologies Inc., also known as Netanomics. Her research combines cognitive science, sociology, and computer science to address complex social and organizational issues. Her most notable research contribution was the establishment of dynamic network analysis (DNA) and the associated theory and methodology for examining large high-dimensional time-variant networks. Her research on DNA has resulted in tools for analyzing and visualizing large-scale dynamic networks and various multiagent simulation systems. She is the developer of a high-dimensional network analysis and visualization system, ORA, that supports network analytics in general for social media and for dynamic and geospatial networks. Her group has also developed tools for extracting sentiment, social, and semantic networks from social media and other textual data (AutoMap); simulating epidemiological models (BioWar); simulating covert networks (DyNet); and simulating changes in beliefs and practice given information campaigns (Construct). She is a fellow of the Institute of Electrical and Electronics Engineers. She holds a Ph.D. in sociology from Harvard University.

Guido Cervone (*Presenter*) is an associate director at the Institute for CyberScience and associate professor of geoinformatics at the Pennsylvania State University. He serves as co-chair of the Research Computing Cyber-Infrastructure Executive Committee. He also holds the appointments of affiliate scientist at the National Center for Atmospheric Research (NCAR) and adjunct faculty at the Lamont-Doherty Earth Observatory, Columbia University. He serves as program co-chair for the Natural Hazards focus group of the American Geophysical Union and chair for the education and outreach advisory board of NCAR. His expertise is in geoinformatics, machine learning, and remote sensing, and his research focuses on the development and application of computational algorithms for the analysis of remote sensing, numerical modeling, and social media spatiotemporal "big data." The main problem domains of his work are related to environmental hazards and renewable energy forecasting. He received his Ph.D. in computational science and informatics and M.S. and B.S. in computer science from George Mason University.

Hsinchun Chen (*Presenter*) is Regents' professor and Thomas R. Brown chair professor in management and technology at the University of Arizona. He recently served as lead program director of the Smart and Connected program at the National Science Foundation (2014–2015), a multiyear multiagency health information technology (IT) research program. He founded the Artificial Intelligence (AI) Lab at the University of Arizona and is a successful IT entrepreneur. His COPLINK/i2 system for security analytics was commercialized and acquired by IBM as its leading government analytics product. He has served as an advisor to major federal research programs and was a scientific counselor of the U.S. National Library of Medicine, the National Library of China, and Academia Sinica (Taiwan). He is a visiting chair professor at several major universities in China and Taiwan. He is internationally known for leading research and development in health analytics and security informatics. He is also a fellow of the Association for Computing Machinery, Institute of Electrical and Electronics Engineers, and the American Association for the Advancement of Science. He received a B.S. from the National Chiao-Tung University in Taiwan, an M.B.A. from the State University of New York at Buffalo, and an M.S. and Ph.D. in information systems from New York University.

Noshir Contractor (*Committee Member*) is Jane S. and William J. White professor of behavioral sciences in the McCormick School of Engineering and Applied Science, the School of Communications, and the Kellogg School of Management, Northwestern University. He is the director of the Science of Networks in Communities research center. He is investigating factors that lead to the formation, maintenance, and dissolution of dynamically linked social and knowledge networks in a wide variety of contexts. He received the National Communication Association Distinguished Scholar Award in 2014 and was elected a fellow of the International Communication Association in 2015. He is the co-founder and chairman of Syndio, which offers to organizations products and services based on network analytics. He holds a B.S. in electrical engineering from the Indian Institute of Technology, Madras, and a Ph.D. in communications from the Annenberg School of Communication, University of Southern California.

Leslie DeChurch (*Presenter*) is professor of communication studies and psychology at Northwestern University. Her research addresses teamwork and leadership in organizations. She is currently investigating the dynamics through which teams form and how these dynamics affect their performance as teams and their ability to work as larger organizational systems (multiteam systems). She is the president of INGRoup (Interdisciplinary Network for Group Research) and fellow of the American Psychological Association, the Association for Psychological Science, and the Society of

Industrial and Organizational Psychology. She holds a Ph.D. in organizational psychology.

Emily Falk (*Committee Member*) is an associate professor of communication at the Annenberg School for Communication, with secondary appointments in psychology and marketing at the University of Pennsylvania. She employs a variety of methods in her research, with a focus on functional magnetic resonance imaging. She has worked to develop a program of research in what she calls "communication neuroscience" to link neural activity (in response to persuasive messages) to behaviors at the individual, group, and population levels. She is also interested in the development of "neural focus groups" to predict the efficacy of persuasive communication at the population level. At present, much of her research focuses on health communication; other areas of interest include political communication, cross-cultural communication, and the spread of culture, social norms, and "sticky" ideas. She received her B.S. in neuroscience from Brown University and her Ph.D. in psychology from the University of California, Los Angeles.

Scott Feld (*Presenter*) is a professor of sociology at Purdue University. His ongoing research interests include causes and consequences of patterns in social networks, processes of individual and collective decision making, and applications of sociology, most recently including innovations in marriage and divorce laws (covenant marriage). He regularly teaches undergraduate and graduate courses on social networks, research methods, and statistics. He received his Ph.D. from the Department of Social Relations at Johns Hopkins University.

Benjamin Golub (*Presenter*) is an assistant professor in the department of economics at Harvard University. His research in economic theory focuses on social and economic networks. His work has examined the dynamics of information and influence around learning and gossip, coordination in organizations, financial contagion, and cooperation and negotiations in complex favor-trading problems, such as pollution reduction. He received his B.S. in mathematics from Caltech and his Ph.D. in economics from Stanford University.

Jesse Hoey (*Presenter*) is an associate professor in the David R. Cheriton School of Computer Science at the University of Waterloo, where he leads the Computational Health Informatics Laboratory. He is also an adjunct scientist at the Toronto Rehabilitation Institute in Toronto, Canada, where he is co-leader of the AI and Robotics Research Team. He works on problems in computational social science, probabilistic and decision theoretic automated reasoning, affective computing, rehabilitation science, and ubiquitous computing. Much of his work has focused on developing systems to help persons with a cognitive disability (e.g., Alzheimer's disease) to engage in activities of daily living. His recent funded research includes a multinational grant from the Trans-Atlantic Partnership to investigate social coordination in online collaborative networks. He was program chair for the 10th European Alliance for Innovation International Conference on Pervasive Computing Technologies for Healthcare and chair of the Technology Professional Interest Area of the Alzheimer's Association International Society to Advance Alzheimer's Research and Treatment. He is a network investigator for the AGEWELL Network of Centers of Excellence. He received his Ph.D. in computer science from the University of British Columbia.

David A. Honey (*Sponsor*) serves as director of science and technology and as assistant deputy director of national intelligence for science and technology in the Office of the Director of National Intelligence. He is responsible for the development of effective strategies, policies, and programs that lead to the successful integration of science and technology capabilities into operational systems. Prior to this assignment, he served as deputy assistant secretary of defense, research, in the Office of the Assistant Secretary of Defense. He was director of the Defense Advanced Research Projects Agency's Strategic Technology Office, director of the Advanced Technology Office, and deputy director and program manager of the Microsystems Technology Office. He is a retired Air Force lieutenant colonel who began his military career as a pilot. He received a Ph.D. in solid state science from Syracuse University.

Kenneth Joseph (*Presenter*) is a postdoctoral fellow at the Network Science Institute, Northeastern University, and a fellow at Harvard's Institute for Quantitative Social Science. He will soon join the computer science department at the University of Buffalo. His research focuses on gaining a better understanding of the dynamics and cognitive representations of stereotypes and prejudice and their interrelationships with sociocultural structure and social interaction. In his work, he leverages a variety of machine learning/natural-language processing methods, agent-based modeling strategies, and sociocognitive theories. He completed his graduate work in the societal computing program at Carnegie Mellon University.

Regina Joseph *(Presenter)* is the founder of Sibylink, an international consultancy based in The Hague, and co-founder of pytho, a U.S.-based decision-science consultancy. Both organizations provide strategic foresight through quantitative forecasting, training programs, and development of digital solutions. She is a superforecaster for the Intelligence Advanced

Research Projects Activity's (IARPA) Aggregative Contingent Estimation Program and was a senior consultant on the IARPA-funded Good Judgment Project research team. She also serves as a member of the faculty at New York University. She is a political scientist whose work and research assist public- and private-sector organizations. Her most recent endeavors include launching the world's first cross-agency forecasting tournament for the government of The Netherlands as part of Sibylink's proprietary strategic foresight training program; the invention of digital tools such as neuertm, a quantified structural analytic technique (patent pending), and InfoRank, an information reliability index; the development of a cyber-threat forecasting platform; and further IARPA-funded research on the development of hybrid human–machine model forecasting systems. She is a Thomas J. Watson fellow and holds a B.A. from Hamilton College and an M.S. from New York University.

Markus Mobius (*Committee Member*) is a principal researcher at Microsoft. His research deals with the economics of social networks. On the theory side, he builds models of learning, coordination, and cooperation within social networks. He is particularly interested in how social networks can generate trust. On the empirical side, he uses a combination of laboratory and field experiments with real social networks to estimate these models. In a second line of research, he has explored how people manage their self-confidence when ego is at stake. He also investigates the use of browsing data to analyze the economics of online news consumption. Formerly, he was an associate professor of economics at Harvard University. He received his B.A. in mathematics and an M.Phil. in economics from Oxford University and his Ph.D. in economics from the Massachusetts Institute of Technology.

James Moody (*Committee Member*) is a professor of sociology at Duke University. He has published extensively in the field of social networks, methods, and social theory. His work has focused theoretically on the network foundations of social cohesion and diffusion, with a particular emphasis on building tools and methods for understanding dynamic social networks. He has used network models to help understand school racial segregation, adolescent health, disease spread, economic development, and the development of scientific disciplines. He holds a B.S. from the University of Oregon and an M.A. and Ph.D. in sociology from the University of North Carolina at Chapel Hill.

Zachary Neal (*Presenter*) is an associate professor of psychology and global urban studies at Michigan State University. His research focuses on multiple scales of urban networks, ranging from microscale social networks among residents within neighborhoods to macroscale economic and transportation networks between cities. He also works to develop new network analytic methods, with a particular focus on bipartite networks and their projections. He was the 2016–2017 recipient of the Freeman Award from the International Network for Social Network Analysis. He received his Ph.D. and M.A. in sociology from the University of Illinois at Chicago.

Carolyn Parkinson (*Presenter*) is an assistant professor of psychology at the University of California, Los Angeles. Her research integrates theory and methods from social psychology, cognitive neuroscience, and social network analysis. Her current work is concerned primarily with better understanding the mental architecture involved in encoding the structure of social networks and the cognitive and behavioral consequences of this structure. By combining the systematic characterization of patterns of real-world social relationships with methods for assessing information processing within individual brains, this line of research is aimed at providing insight into interactions between social networks and human cognition. She received her B.Sc. in psychology from McGill University and her Ph.D. in cognitive neuroscience from Dartmouth College.

Randolph H. Pherson (*Presenter*) has been developing and teaching structured analytic techniques and critical thinking and writing skills to analysts throughout the intelligence, homeland security, and defense communities, as well as in the private sector and overseas. As CEO of Globalytica, LLC, he has developed and taught courses in more than two dozen countries and facilitated more than a dozen strategic foresight workshops, and he recently launched a new online critical thinking course. He also is president of Pherson Associates, which supports U.S. Intelligence Community programs, and founding director of the nonprofit Forum Foundation for Analytic Excellence. He worked as an analyst and manager in the Central Intelligence Agency (CIA) for 28 years, last serving as national intelligence officer (NIO) for Latin America. While at the CIA, he worked on the inspector general's staff, developed a strategic planning process for the agency, and served as deputy executive director. He received the Distinguished Intelligence Medal for his service as NIO for Latin America and the Distinguished Career Intelligence Medal. He holds an A.B. from Dartmouth College and an M.A. in international relations from Yale University.

Paul Sackett (*Decadal Survey Chair*) is Beverly and Richard Fink distinguished professor of psychology and liberal arts at the University of Minnesota. His research interests revolve around various aspects of testing and assessment in workplace, educational, and military settings. He has served as president of the Society for Industrial and Organizational Psychology, as co-chair of the committee producing the Standards for Educational and Psychological Testing, as a member of the National Academies Board on Testing and Assessment, as chair of the American Psychological Association's (APA's) Committee on Psychological Tests and Assessments, and as chair of APA's Board of Scientific Affairs. He holds a Ph.D. in industrial/organizational psychology from Ohio State University.

Alexander Volfovsky (*Presenter*) is an assistant professor of statistical science at Duke University. He joined the department after finishing a National Science Foundation mathematical sciences postdoctoral fellowship at Harvard University. His research concentrates on developing theory and methodological tools for computational social science applications, with a particular focus on high-dimensional data and network analysis. He is interested in assessing fundamental assumptions, such as exchangeability and stochastic equivalence, that underlie many network models, and to this end has developed testing and estimation procedures for complex dependence structures among actors in a network. Recently, he has been working on tools for causal inference and missing-data problems where the existence of networks leads to a breakdown of traditional approaches. His work has been applied to friendship, protein and trade networks, health outcomes, and educational attainment. He received a joint B.S. in mathematics and M.S. in statistics from the University of Chicago and his Ph.D. in statistics from the University of Washington.